HOW TO IN\
THAN THE AVERAGE PRIMATE

Invest the proceeds of your sale commissions wisely.

Michael

HOW TO INVEST BETTER THAN THE AVERAGE PRIMATE

Avoid legalised theft and line your own pockets rather than those of a mercenary sales industry

Michael Barr

Michael Barr Publishing
19 Poulton Road
Carleton
Poulton-Le-Fylde
FY6 7NH
Tel: +44(0) 01253 885844
Website: www.michaelbarr.org.uk

First published in Great Britain in 2010
©Michael Barr 2010

The right of Michael Barr to be identified as the author of this work has been asserted in accordance with the Copyright, Designs and Patents Act, 1988.

ISBN: 978-0-9565244-0-9

All rights reserved. No part of this publication may be reproduced, stored in a retrieval system, or transmitted in any form or by any means, electronic, mechanical, photocopying, recording, or otherwise, without permission in writing from the author.

The personal views and opinions expressed in this publication are those of the author.

This publication is designed to provide accurate and authoritative information in regard to the subject matter covered. While the author has used his best efforts in preparing this book, he makes no representations or warranties with respect to the accuracy or completeness of the contents and specifically disclaims any implied warranties of merchantability or fitness for a particular purpose. No warranty may be created or extended by sales representatives or written sales materials. The advice and strategies contained herein may not be suitable for the readers' situation and a consultation with a competent professional is recommended. Neither the publisher nor the Author shall be liable for any loss of profit or any other commercial damages, including but not limited to special, incidental, consequential, or other damages.

British Library Cataloguing in Publication data
A CIP catalogue reference for this book can be obtained from the British Library

Printed and bound in Great Britain by
CPI Antony Rowe, Chippenham and Eastbourne

"How many a man has created a new era in his life from the reading of a book?"

—Henry David Thoreau.

The title of this book was inspired by a controlled experiment, in which chimpanzees made random investment selections by throwing darts at the Wall Street Journal. Their selections outperformed those made by the majority of professional fund managers.

The thought of a chimp successfully moonlighting as a fund manager, whilst mildly amusing, also serves to expose the shortcomings of the fund management industry.

In memory of Betty Young who chose not to give me up and to Myfanwy and George Barr who offered a loving home to a young boy.

Contents

Why you should read this book	11
Foreword	13
A Brief Overview	15
How to build a reliable investment portfolio	16
Glossary	18

SECTION 1: What you must know before investing   21

We are encouraged to invest in a state of confusion	23
Falling stars and how investors suffer from poor advice	40
Banking is no different to car sales	47
Would you lose your home in a fire?	55
The not so perfect investments	63
The outrageous cost of investing	66
Commission and the lure of free advice	68
A summary of the bad practices that cost you money	73

SECTION 2: Planning and understanding the risks   75

Avoiding death on the operating table – have a plan	77
Living to the age of 100	80
Inflation – we should change our perception of risk	86
Investing for a millionaire lifestyle -1980 to 2008	90
The stock market's future	96
Managing your own share portfolio	99

SECTION 3: Stock market strategies   103

Picking the best time to invest	105
How do professional investors work?	116
Charts and the search for patterns	119

SECTION 4: Build your own portfolio — 123

Achieving success is easier than a round of golf — 125
How to beat the professional investor — 130
Plan your short term savings first — 132
Your Portfolio — 133
The $50,000 question – how did we do? — 140
Case studies – the first year — 148
The first year review — 154

SECTION 5: The value of good advice — 159

The value of good advice — 161
How to spot the wrong adviser — 163
The successful DIY investor is a rare breed — 166
More advanced investment strategies — 169

Appendices — 177

Buying your own index investment funds — 179
   Employer pension schemes — 182
   The Child Trust Fund — 184
It is harder than you think to beat the average return — 185
The tax-free ISA allowance — 190
The industry's poor record of treating customers fairly — 191
The most common toxic investments — 193
Reliable information comes from the academic world — 207
It takes 16 years to prove investment skill — 215
List of Charts and data sources — 228
Useful contacts and addresses — 231

Acknowledgements — 235
About the author — 236
Index — 237

Why you should read this book

THE REGULATION of independent financial advice has increased and the effect has been to restrict the availability of professional financial advice to the relatively wealthy. Meanwhile, the rest of us face the mercenary sales tactics used by banks, insurance companies and independent financial sales.

This book will help you to understand how to build your own very simple but effective investment portfolio in a way not possible in the UK until recent times. You will learn:

- how to invest with the odds in your favour
- how to avoid making costly mistakes
- what really matters when investing
- how to review what you are doing already
- how to get back on track
- If you prefer to work with an adviser, you will learn how a good professional works

If you prefer to work with an adviser, you will learn how to recognise an ethical professional and you will never again be misled by a financial salesperson, or reply to an advertisement for a bad investment.

Do not worry if you have no previous knowledge of investing. I will assume that you have no prior knowledge other than what you may have read in newspapers, or heard in conversations with friends, family and colleagues. Each chapter of the book presents a simple message. Detailed information for the more inquisitive investor can be found in the appendix.

This book will give you the knowledge to take control of your investments, and to cut your investment costs by three-quarters. If you do not have the time or inclination to run your own portfolio, or your affairs are complicated, you will learn what questions to ask when selecting a good adviser.

Foreword

I ENJOYED WINNING my National Awards in the 1990's. I gained some great publicity, the media courted me, I wrote articles and there were profitable speaking engagements.

Looking back, I do not see these awards as a career highlight at all, because I had only discovered how to impress a committee, a panel of judges, and sponsors who had a vested interest in maintaining the status quo. There was very little originality in my submissions and impressing a few of my peers did nothing that would improve the public's access to good investments.

My career changed for the better when I understood it was possible to make real improvements to the investments offered to clients. It still seems to me that most advisers long to preserve what they have, which is often only profitable for them. I see them rolling their eyes when presented with new ideas and standards, and their attitude is to fight against change. They put too much store in the past, which is like driving down the motorway using only the rear mirror.

I believe that the typical investor is quietly looking to rebel against what is generally on offer, but they need to formulate a cause before they can force the professionals to tear up their old ideas. Investors know that their situation will not improve until they have access to better advice.

I hope this book is not just a pleasantly acceptable piece of work. During my research, I have noticed that genuinely good and practical investment ideas do not arrive very often and great ideas are something of a once in a generation event. For this reason I invite constructive criticism and suggestions, so that I can improve on the strategies I describe. Improvements could mean beating the typical investor eight or nine times out of ten, rather than only three-quarters of the time, which is my present expectation over a ten-year run.

A Brief Overview

"There is no coming to consciousness without pain"
—Karl Jung

What is legalised theft?

'Legalised theft' is a description I first used over 20 years ago. I was appalled by the standards of advice given to investors who mistakenly believed that they could trust the banks, insurance companies and so-called independent advisers. The advice they received came at a heavy price, in the form of obscene rates of commission, which did not have to be disclosed. Other than the disclosure of commission, little has changed since then.

Although the industry is regulated, customers continue to be sold poor investment products, and high charges stunt the growth of the investments that could otherwise have been profitable.

There is a lot of mercenary activity in the UK financial services industry, and this is covered in the early chapters of this book. The good news is that there are also a growing number of companies offering very good investment products, and a growing number of educated and ethical advisers. This book will help you to identify them.

How to build a reliable investment portfolio

THE METHOD of investment I advocate will not only save you the exorbitant fees that may be charged by a professional fund manager, but will also be more consistent in terms of reliability and results. This is not an exaggeration, but an observation that is both statistically and mathematically accurate.

Investing is not just about stocks and shares – a variety of low risk investments are vital for a balanced investment strategy. When deciding what to include in a portfolio, you must avoid dangerous investments masquerading as low risk opportunities.

The investment approach I recommend is known as 'index investing'. Some refer to it as 'passive investing'. A passive investment strategy is the opposite of an active one. Although the term 'passive' has some negative connotations, it is the smart way to invest. A better description might be 'reliable investing'.

An experienced gardener once told me why my houseplants looked ill. The reason, he said, "was an absence of neglect". He examined my plants, and confirmed I was overwatering them, spending too much money on fertilisers, and that this behaviour was killing them. The best approach is to set them up properly, keep them out of the harsh sunlight, and then they will look after themselves.

The recommended maintenance was simply to keep an eye on them, pay them a little common sense attention, and then they will thrive and bloom wonderfully without any other help from me. An additional piece of advice was to steer clear of certain exotic plants as they are expensive, demand high maintenance, and the results are often disappointing.

Indexing, or passive investing, is successful because you buy a good investment and give it a chance to grow and bloom. You do not have to buy and sell investments on a regular basis. Most investors are encouraged to trade actively, or to buy specialised managed funds, which are the equivalent of exotic plants. Too often the results are disappointing and the price is too high.

The methods described in this book are not new, but it was not possible to build such a portfolio in the UK until recently. In the USA, investors have had an advantage for years. Now we have the opportunity to have our turn.

It is perfectly feasible for a beginner to construct a simple but effective balanced portfolio, which offers the prospects of better results than the portfolios most professionals recommend.

New investors will not struggle as the successful investment method is explained in stages. The chapters are planned so you do not have too much to take in at once. This is important, as it gives you the opportunity to understand one concept, which naturally leads to the next.

Glossary

Jargon has been kept to the bare minimum in this book.

Asset class – a group of investments that tends to behave in the same way when conditions change. The main asset classes are equities, gilts, bonds and cash deposits

Equities – stock market investments. An equity is a share in a company, or a stock, as in stocks and shares.

Gilts – when the Government borrows money it issues gilts. They promise to pay a guaranteed income and return your capital at maturity. Index-linked gilts have a return linked to the rate of inflation.

Bonds – when a company wishes to borrow money it either borrows from a bank, in a way familiar to us all, or it issues a bond. A bond usually promises to return your capital at maturity, in preference to shareholders, and pays a fixed rate of interest.

Investment Bonds – these are also known as insurance bonds. These are contracts issued by insurance companies and they are widely sold by IFA's and banks. The use of the word 'Bond' is confusing because the investment may have no connection with bonds as described above. The entire investment may be in property, equities, or a mix of different investments. Generally, the contracts are an expensive way to buy investments. They also come in the form of with-profit bonds and property bonds.

Managed funds – these are a way of investing in equities, gilts, commercial property and bonds. Each fund has a manager and the objective is to run a diverse portfolio for investors. There are different names for them including ETF's, mutual funds, unit trusts, investment trusts, OEIC's, investment bonds, and iShares. There are versions run for personal pension funds and insurance company funds.

SECTION 1

WHAT YOU MUST KNOW BEFORE INVESTING

We are encouraged to invest in a state of confusion

"Can't we get you on Mastermind, Sybil? Specialist subject – the bleedin' obvious!"
—Basil Fawlty, 1975

UMA THURMAN, Steven Spielberg, Zsa Zsa Gabor, Kevin Bacon and Ringo Starr. What do all these celebrities have in common?

Just like HSBC, the Royal Bank of Scotland, and Abbey National they all lost money in the biggest financial fraud of modern times. Bernard Madoff, who currently resides in prison, stripped these celebrities of millions of dollars and conned UK banks out of an estimated $5 billion.

All Madoff's clients were clearly confused. The investment strategy he used "was certain to give a regular 12% a year". He called it the "split strike conversion". When I first heard the term, I harboured a vague suspicion that it somehow related to ten-pin bowling.

Many industry insiders would maintain that before investing $5 billion, you should at least have a rough idea of what will be done with your money. I don't know what a split strike conversion is, and more importantly, none of the victims knew either. Presumably, the advisers of the above celebrities must have told their clients that they knew how a 'split strike conversion' worked.

This kind of fraud reveals a lot about the way we can behave when making investment decisions. We allow ourselves to invest without understanding what we are buying and we believe what we are told without seeing any facts or evidence.

At a different level, highly questionable advice is served up to customers of the UK financial institutions. Investors are losing money because they are being fed misleading information. We allow ourselves to be the victims of 'legalised theft' – a term I use to describe the poor and expensive advice dished out by the UK financial services industry on a daily basis. They manage to pull this off with the help of misdirection and misinformation.

Most people receive investment advice in a sales environment. They are weighed down with so much information at the point of sale that they are unable to think straight. We are driven to a state of confusion. And, at the very time when our heads should be clear, when the final decision is made and we sign on the dotted line, people still do not understand what is going to happen to their money.

The sales literature is such that you do not take in much that is useful at all, and the decisions we are persuaded to make are generally based on falsehoods. A life insurance and investment salesman once told me the financial regulations helped him to close his investment sales quickly. He said, "The client is overwhelmed by so much unnecessary jargon that they don't stand a chance." Getting excited as he talked about the way he manipulated customers he said, "They never asked any questions because they were made to feel stupid. The commission figures and expenses were all there to be seen in black and white, but they either couldn't find them, or when they did, they couldn't understand them."

What an unpleasant way to earn a living – working in a way deliberately designed to ensure a customer cannot see the wood for the trees.

Investors are being short-changed by this poor behaviour. You must never, no matter what, ever make an investment unless you understand the principles of what is happening to your money. You do not have to understand every detail, but you should find some independent evidence to support the advice you are being given.

Don't be confused by past performance

When you are sold an investment, you are given a risk warning along the following lines:

> "Past performance is not a guide to future performance. The value of investments and the income from them can fluctuate and investors may not get back the amount originally invested"

When you think about this statement for one moment, isn't it so obvious that it has absolutely no value? It is symptomatic of the poor thinking in the financial services industry. If past performance were such a good guide, then financial planning would be easy. The best stocks and shares and the best interest rates on offer would always be the best. It would be the same as expecting the same teams to always win the Premier league, the same nations to win the World

Cup, and no betting on the results would take place because we would all know what to expect.

In reality, the world is constantly changing. The teams that got relegated from Premier league football cannot get relegated again because they're no longer in the Premier league, and the teams that got promoted cannot win in the same way again, because they are no longer in the same division.

The table below shows that past performance does not repeat. At the end of 2003 the best performing fund out of 149 funds was the worst performing fund out of 239 funds five years later. Only one of the top ten funds was in the top 50 five years later. The one consistent fund, run by Fidelity, has since had a change of manager.

Do not judge an investment by its past performance

Fund Name	Jan 1999 – Dec 2003		Jan 2004 – Dec 2008	
	Rank	Total Return	Rank	Total Return
Rathbone Special Sits Income	1	24.23	239	-10.52
GAM UK Diversified inc	2	21.84	112	2.43
Fidelity Special Situations	3	16.74	7	6.95
Cavendish Opportunities Rtl	4	14.36	236	-6.92
Artemis UK Growth	5	13.27	172	0.98

Marlborough UK Equity Growth	6	12.92	229	-3.60
Solus UK Special Situations Income	7	11.86	182	0.55
Schoder Recovery Income	8	11.82	61	3.53
Blackrock UK Special Sits A Inc	9	10.95	24	5.45
Artemis Capital	10	8.79	161	1.34
Total Number of Funds in the sector		149		239

Why am I stating the bleedin' obvious? It's because the investment industry actively ignores its own risk warning that *"past performance is no guide to future performance"*. The industry uses past performance as a sales tool all the time. Often it is subtly done, but there is no doubt – they suggest, imply, hint or simply allow you to jump to a conclusion; that what an investment has achieved in the past is repeatable.

Why do we fall for the sales patter that leads us astray? This becomes clear when you look at the way we all tend to evaluate and process information before making a decision.

The lucky tosser who tells you it is skill

Let's imagine a room full of 100 people. We ask them to toss a coin, then to stand up if they flip heads or to sit down if they flip tails. It is reasonable to expect 50 to remain standing after the first toss. We ask the 50 standing to keep tossing, then to sit down when they have tails, so that after five tosses we would expect to still see three of them standing. We would also say these three had a lucky run of heads.

The three who remain standing are categorically *not* skilful. In fact, if we started with a town of 100,000 people it would take about 15 tosses to arrive at three very lucky coin tossers. No one would dream of claiming there was any skill. They simply had a very good run of luck.

Now let's imagine a second similar situation, but this time there are 100 fund managers who all claim to be experts in the stock market. Of course they all claim to be the best, and they all claim the ability to outperform the average UK stock market investor.

Any race has winners and losers and those in between. After the first year of investing, about half of the fund managers will be above the market average and half will be below the average. As with the coin tossers, three of them look good after five years, which is exactly the result you would expect – it cannot be any other way.

But this time, when the three claim to be experts rather than lucky, we believe them. We believe them because they must be clever people to have beaten the stock market average over the last five years. We see it as an achievement. Why do we not just consider them to be lucky? The only difference is the way in which we judge what happened – we assess the coin tosser to be lucky, and the fund manager to be skilful.

It is entirely reasonable to expect skill from a fund manager. London, New York, and all the rest of the world's capital cities have buildings packed with financial analysts. Between them they spend hundreds of millions of pounds on research to investigate which companies to buy or sell. Surely, all these resources at the hands of so many experts and eggheads must pay off? Well, all the evidence available says it doesn't. The competition for information is so intense that no one gains an advantage for long enough to make it count. This makes the market so efficient that it is impossible to have any information advantage over anyone else.

Another problem for investors, which is almost impossible for you to discover on your own, is the fact that the history of investment funds is constantly rewritten. What seems to be a record of the past is often not at all accurate as the figures are fiddled.

A 'smoke and mirrors' tactic that some fund managers often employ is to get rid of the poor performing funds by closing them down. The surviving banks, investment and insurance companies often have poor results because of their rotten investment policies.

Unfortunately for their customers, they are allowed to airbrush their mistakes from history, bury their bad news, so it disappears without trace as an unrecorded statistic.

In recent years, the rate of disappearing funds has accelerated, and remarkably, the Financial Services Authority (the FSA) actually allows this tardy sort of behaviour to take place. Published research suggests the average professionally managed fund in the UK market underperforms the FTSE All Share index by 2% a year[1].

What a difference 2% makes		
£100,000 invested	5 years	10 years
5%	£127,628	£162,888
7%	£140,255	£196,715

1 "Are UK fund investors achieving fund rates of return? An examination of the differences between UK fund returns and UK Investors' returns." Lukas Schneider July 2007.

Most advisers and salespeople in the industry ignore these failures because it conflicts with their sales philosophy. They are trained to sell investments that offer the promise of 'outperformance'. They are entrenched in their behaviour, and why change when the customers are trapped by the attractive ideas of past performance and manager skill?

When you seek investment advice there is a general pattern. It is one of being told that you should be aiming to 'outperform' and 'beat' the markets. If you fall for it you are going to be disappointed, because it is likely your manager will not be a lucky one.

> **Fund managers hide their failures**
>
> Morningstar, the research and fund-rating agency, keeps records of the performance of UK investment funds. It noted a change in its database for the five-year period ending December 1996. By the end of 1998, two years after the period ended, there should have been no change to the history of the fund mangers performance figures, but they had somehow retrospectively increased. The average return of the UK Large Value sector had increased by 1.1% a year, and the UK Small Cap Growth had increased by 1.7% a year. How could history have changed like this?
>
> It was the result of managers closing their poor performing funds, which then disappeared from the records. When you see the past performance records of funds in databases and in sales literature, you are seeing only the survivors. You are definitely not seeing the entire history of events. In the academic world this is known as

survivorship bias', and this bias has become very significant in the last 10 years.[2]

In this period we have seen the disappearance of a number of failed insurance companies and banks.

Less than one in a hundred perform well

Active fund managers must achieve an investment return through luck or skill, after taking a fee, to prove their worth to clients. A study[3] reviewed fund manager returns after charges between 1990 and 2006 and split the managers in three groups.

The first group turned out to be totally unskilled and this lot accounted for nearly one quarter of all the fund managers. So, one in four managers were unable to pick stocks well enough to recover their trading costs and expenses. However, these unskilled managers have a relatively long average life expectancy of nearly 13 years. They can only exist if ignorant investors are supporting them. Why else would you pay a high fee for nothing?

The second group, accounting for three-quarters of fund

---

2 In a 2009 report the FSA said it had approved 808 changes to existing investment schemes during 2008, an increase of 10% on the previous year. Many of these changes involved the reorganisation and rationalisation of retail investment funds.

S&P reported that 27% of the 2,154 US equity funds in existence five years ago have merged or liquidated as of June 30, 2009.

Morningstar reported that 10% of small growth funds have disappeared in just the first six months of 2009.

3 False discoveries in mutual fund performance: Measuring luck in estimated alphas – Laurent Barras, O. Scaillet, Russ Wermers, University of Maryland and Swiss Finance Institute, May 2008.

managers, had just enough skill to cover their trading costs and other expenses. Unfortunately, they delivered no benefits to investors but the managers got their high fees.

The third group did perform well, and it outperformed the market after fees. It could have been down to skill, or it could have been down to luck, but they would have been difficult to find because this group represented less than one percent – only 0.6% of all fund managers.

Is the industry really confused or just cynical?

The social anthropologist Ernest Gellner wrote about the 'unifying power of falsehood'. Truths are available to all, and thereby become trivial, but belief in an absurdity demands greater commitment. Collective commitment to an absurdity can thereby become a powerful unifying force.

There is a huge body of scientific evidence in existence to tell us how to invest wisely, but it is not that easy to find. This is knowledge that the financial services industry would rather not share with you. If too many of us begin to understand the truth, and end their involvement with the collective delusion, it will be very inconvenient for most fund management groups in the industry.

In my opinion, very few investment advisers in the UK seem to have a good understanding of what a successful investment strategy looks like. As a result, far too many of their customers end up with the wrong investments.

It is possible that the investment industry is in denial. It is perhaps more likely that it prefers to maintain the status quo to retain the high level of commissions and charges being skimmed off customer's funds.

Often, however, industry personnel seem to be victims of their own propaganda. Some advisers must see the evidence that shows they are of no benefit to their clients, and they ignore it. The academic evidence they reject is a rejection of statistics, probability and logic. Then again, when it comes to selling, it is sometimes prudent for them to disregard certain facts.

If an adviser tells you something that contradicts this book, then you should demand to see the evidence that such advice is based on. Only rigorous academic evidence will do. Anyone who presents an argument counter to the message of this book will ultimately be found to be lacking.

Parliament and the FSA, at least, do not support the idea that past performance shows us how to invest in the future.

When giving evidence to the Treasury Committee in May 2006[4], two leading executives of the FSA were questioned about the merits of actively managed funds bearing in mind the additional costs involved. The background to their appearance was an examination of the proposed new National Pension Savings Scheme.

The FSA executives made a clear statement. There is no evidence that actively managed funds perform better than passive funds.

---

4 House of Commons, Minutes of Evidence ordered by the House of Commons, Minutes of Evidence ordered by the House of Commons, printed 18 May 2006.

Fund managers wreck pension funds

"Professionals in other fields, like dentists, bring a lot to the Layman, but people get nothing for their money from professional money managers."

—Warren Buffett

The word that should stand out from this quotation, by arguably the most successful investor of all time, is 'nothing'. Some of the most successful funds – in terms of sales – performed very badly for the actual investors.

A list of the 10 worst big retail pension funds follows. Each had more than £1bn invested in them at the time.

TEN POOR PENSION FUNDS

Abbey Equity	Scottish Life Property
Friends Provident UK Equity	HSBC Life (UK) Pen Balanced
Scottish Life Managed	Lincoln Balanced Managed 3
Clerical Medical Balanced	Lloyds TSB Managed
Phoenix Life Exempt Managed	Barclays Life Managed 2

These 10 funds held about £20,000,000,000 of investor's money – £20bn. The Abbey Equity and Friends Provident UK Equity funds, for example, had £3bn between them and the performances over a five-year period to the end of 2008 were dire. They earned less than a deposit account which was less than a total of 10% over five years.

Had these stock market fund managers done their job well, they should have earned a return at least equal to the FTSE All share Index, which is a profit of over 22%. These two funds denied the investors a profit of 12% over a five-year period.

What were the fund managers involved doing? They tried to outperform the market, and in the process they made a series of bad decisions.

The advisers who sold these funds persuaded investors to put £20bn of their hard earned savings into a black hole. Over £2bn of pension money was lost by these two funds alone in only 5 years.

The regulators do not believe in past performance

In the year 2000, the FSA published a paper[5] with the following key statement in the executive summary:

"This paper presents evidence on whether information on the past investment performance of unit trusts can be useful to retail investors. The conclusions are important for investors who may be unsure of the value of information on past investment performance when choosing a fund. The issue is also important to the FSA in considering what information to publish in its comparative information tables.

A number of researchers have examined whether past investment performance repeats. The conclusion from an examination of this literature is that repeat performance (if there is any) is both small in the size of effect and short lived. Repeat performance (persistency) is most evident for smaller poorly performing funds but the degree of persistency remains low. The conclusion from studies of UK unit trusts, and the more reliable of US studies, is that retail investors could not usefully exploit information on past performance."

---

5 Past Imperfect? The performance of UK equity managed funds by Mark Rhodes

> *"This also provides an opportunity to examine further the apparent end in the relationship between past and subsequent investment performance. The results concurred with the earlier analyses in finding that there was no persistency in the performance of managed funds after 1987. There was evidence of repeat performance before this point but it would be misleading to suggest that retail investors could use this finding in the present day."*

The Australian Financial Services Authority published a similar paper soon after this in 2002, and a revised version in 2003[6]. This report was also very thorough, and it examined research conducted in the US and the UK. It concluded:

"Past performance seems to be, at best, a weak and unreliable predictor of future good performance over the medium to long term. About half the studies found no correlation at all between good past and good future performance. Where persistence was found, this was more frequently in the shorter-term, (one to two years) than in the longer term. The longer-term comparison may be more relevant to the typical periods over which consumers hold managed funds.

- *More studies seem to find that bad past performance increased the probability of future bad performance.*
- *Where persistence was found, the "out-performance" margin tended to be small.*

Where studies found persistence, some specifically reported that frequent swapping to best performing funds would not be an effective strategy, due to the cost of swapping.

---

6 A Review of the Research on the Past Performance of Managed Funds. Report prepared for the Australian Securities and Investment Commission By the Funds Management Research Centre (FMRC) Of the Securities Industry Research Centre of the Asia Pacific (SIRCA)

These two detailed studies, one commissioned by the FSA and the second commissioned by the Australian equivalent of the FSA, concluded past performance is no guide to the future.

When the FSA paper was issued it was widely reported, and a shocked industry offered little in terms of a logical response. In the long run, very little has changed. The majority of the industry carries on as before and spends massively on advertising and perpetuating the myth of past performance having some value.

The UK and Australian authorities have never issued any evidence that indicates past performance is helpful. This is because past performance is absolutely useless when planning ahead.

The gifted few

What about those people who are genuinely skilled and gifted? It would be wrong to ignore the fact that some people have demonstrated that they have the skill to outperform the markets. Inconveniently, these people are very small in number, and it is not possible to identify them in advance. By the time they are identified as skilful, they are likely to be near the end of their careers.

There is also a history that suggests it is a bad idea to try and follow gifted fund managers when they move on. When they are placed in a different environment, the 'magic' often disappears.

Don't be confused by forecasting

Small talk in Britain revolves around the weather. We love talking about the weather forecast, and how often it is wrong. Although it is often wrong, we still have the expectation that it will be right. People walk to work dressed in summer clothes, and they arrive soaking wet. The weather forecast said it was going to be a summer day, so the umbrella is left at home. No matter how many times this happens, people still hold the weather forecast in high regard.

If we are going on holiday next week and it's raining this week, some people become gloomy, expecting their holiday will be a washout. But the weather this week rarely has anything to do with next week's weather.

I spend a lot of time walking in the Lake District, and it is a good idea to check the weather forecast before setting off. Unfortunately, mountain weather forecasts can be very unreliable. Mountain rescue teams will tell you that most callouts are the result of people not having proper clothing. They hear a good forecast and assume the weather will turn out as predicted, despite the forecast being wrong innumerable times before. The sensible approach is to prepare for the worst so that you won't be caught unawares.

There was a spell when the mountain weather forecast was completely wrong for about 10 consecutive weeks. It always rained when the forecast had been good, sometimes on a biblical scale. A friend of mine said – in all seriousness – "Never mind, the forecast is sunshine all next week". We cannot help ourselves!

In exactly the same way, we believe those who predict the stock market. Analysts tell us which investment is going to be the next big thing, or when the stock market is going to collapse. And, just like the weather forecast, we actually believe it. We love to be told what to expect in the future, and this makes us all vulnerable.

Stock and property market predictions are essentially guesswork. Sometimes, of course, we make the right guess, but it's certainly not a good idea to base your investment choices on guesswork. We should recognise the fact that predictions are often wrong, both in meteorology and the stock market.

Studying past performance and a belief in the value of forecasting are two sides of the same coin. If a fund manager is having a lucky run they are assumed to have good forecasting skills as the two are connected. After all, you must have been able to forecast the future to have achieved your good past performance.

Whatever you do, do not fall for any of this nonsense. Forecasting the future would be a useful ability, but regretfully there is no evidence to suggest that anyone can accurately do this. Predicting the future is best left to astrologists and fortune tellers.

Falling stars and how investors suffer from poor advice

> *"This message (that attempting to beat the market is futile) can never be sold on Wall Street because it is in effect telling stock analysts to drop dead."*
> —Paul Samuelson, Ph.D., Nobel Prize Laureate

How investors suffer when the luck runs out

THE ABERDEEN technology fund was one of the biggest selling funds during the late 1990's. It attracted a total of 200,000 investors who saw the enviable past performance of the fund, and expected it to be repeated. The fund managers generated massive profits for themselves and their shareholders. However, as often happens with specialist funds, its fortunes quickly reversed. It lost 82% of its value.

The UK's fastest-growing investment group at the time was 'New Star' and it bought the troubled fund in 2000, bringing the hope of better times for the investors. A deal was done involving six Aberdeen unit trusts (Aberdeen was in difficulty when some of its other funds had to be liquidated, and investors were only compensated when the FSA stepped in).

New Star had launched only two years earlier and its

outspoken chairman said the group's primary objective was to provide its investors with superior investment returns across a broad range of asset classes.

An early failure was the New Star Special Situations fund. It lost over 15%, which is not the special situation that most people had in mind when they bought it. During this time it would have been reasonable for a UK stock market fund to make 2% or 3%. To erase the poor performance of the fund from industry records, it was merged with the better performing New Star UK Alpha fund in February 2008.

Unfortunately by 2008, five years after the Aberdeen deal, the majority of the New Star flagship funds had performed abysmally. Two out of three were in the bottom 25% of funds in their sector, and there were several 'black holes'. The history-erasing UK Alpha fund lost one quarter of its value, the Select Opportunities fund more than halved in value, and the UK Growth fund lost 45%. Its biggest retail fund, the UK Property fund also underperformed, but the worst performer was the unfortunately named 'Hidden Value' fund. The fund lost more than half of its value in one year.

The death of New Star

The Henderson Group completed the acquisition of New Star in 2009. Existing fund managers were either sacked, or they moved on. The New Star managers had been billed as highly skilled with 'formidable reputations'. The reality was that the managers were lucky, and then their luck ran out.

It is estimated that New Star had about 300,000 private investors who ploughed billions into its funds between 2001 and 2008. On top of the losses these investors suffered, they had all paid substantial fees for the mismanagement of their money.

One of the fund managers earned £4.7[7] million in 2007, and many others at New Star earned in a year what some people would consider their total career earnings. Most people would happily pay fees for the skill to produce a reliable market beating performance, but in reality this skill is not there to be bought.

Where did the advice to jump into New Star originate? Many financial advisers firmly backed New Star when it launched in 2001. They recommended the new funds to clients with the promise of outperformance, and I expect a lot of commission was earned.

The Daily Telegraph questioned some of the advisers who had been invited to the New Star launch party in 2001, and who recommended New Star to clients. What were they advising their clients to do when it failed? The table below examines their responses.

What they said[8]	The authors' interpretation
"The bond funds have been beaten up- they took on a bit too much risk too early. But they are in good company"	The low risk funds turned out to be high-risk funds and clients lost a lot of money, which was a shock. However, they are no worse off than a lot of our other clients who are in the other poor funds we picked.

7 Source: Reuters – UK New Star fund manager Pease's pay rises by 270 pct Fri Apr 20, 2007.
8 An extract from the Daily Telegraph: original copy by Paul Farrow Published: 2:05PM GMT 01 Dec 2008

"My preference is New Star Sterling Bond – holding bonds with a lot of potential. It's painful if you're already an investor, but for new money these funds have obvious 'bounceability'.	This low-risk fund has produced poor returns. If you are prepared to invest in a high-risk fund, which was originally sold as a low-risk fund, there is a chance it might come good.
"Under normal circumstances we look at our system of rating, but these are not normal circumstances, and we have to adapt to the economic environment that we are now experiencing.	Our rating system does not work. We're not sure what to do next.
"Equity Income and Higher Income – have been battered and aren't rated, ... higher-yielding shares are likely to be increasingly sought after in 2009."	The income funds we selected have been downgraded by the rating agencies because they are very bad. We are guessing that riskier shares might do well next year.
" The New Star funds we recommend have, in the past, had an excellent track record, although they have suffered in current market conditions... alternatives we recommend to the above funds are ..."	We based our fund recommendations on past performance. This did not turn out well for our clients. However, based on the commission we will earn when we switch our clients' funds, we are again prepared to recommend on the basis of past performance.

"We do not currently recommend any New Star funds. Until very recently the International Property fund was our preferred way of gaining exposure to international property, but in the light of the suspension of dealing in this fund we opted to impose an embargo on new monies for this fund.	It was a mistake to recommend new Star funds. As a lot of our clients cannot get their money out of the property fund. We are going to tell them to leave it where it is.
"Anyone holding the UK Growth, Higher Income or Sterling Bond fund should, in our view, reassess these investments.	A lot of our clients were given disastrous advice. When they calm down we will tell them to cut their losses.

The New Star story is not unique. Many fund management groups are merged into others with the effect of removing the fund management mistakes from historical records.

The victims of the New Star saga were not the multimillionaire fund managers and their bosses, but the customers who invested their money in good faith, and suffered spectacular losses.

Astonishingly, New Star's former chief investment officer confirmed he had always believed in passive investing.[9] Miller, who apparently earned £3.3 million in 2003 as the Chief Investment Officer and manager of New Star's Hedge Fund, confirmed he invested his own money in index trackers. He did this whilst earning massive fees and bonuses for gambling on the market with other people's money.

Miller said at the time *"In every single study you see the average manager underperforms. Very few have consistent*

---

9 Published in the Citywire's 'New Model Adviser'.

outperformance through their stock selection. You are better off not taking that risk." He also went on to say, "... *The cost would also be lower than the high charges incurred by traditional active managers, which are often hidden from investors.*"

So there you have it, straight from the horse's mouth.

Any fund manager without skill can have a run of success during good market conditions, and the run of luck is used in promotional posters and brochures. Unfortunately, it is all too easy to fall for sales patter that revolves around past performance, and the related propaganda issued by banks, insurance companies and the media.

A lucky fund manager will attract a lot of new money. Inevitably, though, luck runs out and the money then flows to the next lucky manager.

The role of the media

Newspapers have to fill the financial pages even when there is relatively little to report. The only way to fill all these pages is by printing just about anything that can be found to write about. There is no correlation between the size of a financial section and the wisdom it contains. It seems that any 'expert opinion', or comment about which way the stock market is going will do because there are a lot of column inches to fill.

If the market has been going up there will be plenty of stories suggesting it is about to go down, and if the market has been going down there will usually be plenty of column inches devoted to why it should keep going down. It can be very difficult to separate fact from fiction.

There is no doubt in my mind that articles relating to forecasting dominate the papers because they capture our imagination. There are often more negative than positive articles, and if you followed all the advice you would nearly always be a seller, and miss the good market recoveries.

Once you realise that most newspaper columns, purporting to offer investment advice, should be regarded as a form of entertainment, you are on the right track. Some academics refer to these pages as 'investment pornography'.

Every year, between Christmas and New Years Eve, popular fund managers are asked to forecast the year ahead, and some publications will print the results without any comment or criticism. Some of these experts generously share their top tips and make their forecasts. Most of them seem quite happy to be quoted, despite the fact that their predictions usually turn out to be wrong.

In my opinion, these kinds of articles should come with a health warning. An investor may write a piece that essentially summarises a lucky experience, of using a certain method of trading and then passing on a few tips. It would be reasonable to have a footnote recommending most readers to exercise a cautious approach when trying to copy it, because it could also be a potentially wealth-destroying strategy.

Banking is no different to car sales

"Go where you will in business parts, or meet who you like of business men, it is the same story and the same lament. Dishonesty, untruth, and what may in plain English be termed mercantile swindling within the limits of the law, exists on all sides and on every quarter."
—Charles Dickens, writing for the *Temple Bar Journal*, 1866.

THESE ARE difficult times for the surviving banks and insurance companies and they are desperate to maintain the status quo. The status quo involves selling high-risk investment packages that can be bad for the investor, but lucrative for the organisation and the sales team.

Imagine you are going to treat yourself to a new car. You read some magazines, do some internet research, ask your friends for an opinion, and visit a few showrooms. For the sake of argument, let's say you decide to buy a Ford.

The last part of your car-buying journey is to visit the Ford showroom to decide on the model and specification. As you produce your cheque book, the salesman, who's done a fine job, puts his hand on your shoulder and says, "Look, you are obviously a hard-working person and have saved up to buy a new car. It just so happens that my mother has just bought a Nissan, and to be honest it's a much better car than this Ford. Why don't you go down to the Nissan garage now as you can get a really good deal at the moment?"

Of course, this will never happen unless the salesman's mother works for Nissan! In reality, as soon as you walk through the showroom door, the sales people are going to tell you why their brand of car is the best for you, and then try to secure a quick sale.

You are not going to be shown a 'What car?' magazine or a 'Which?' report showing you that their car is merely average. But they will have found at least one report that is very convincing about the quality of their vehicles and how they can improve your life.

When you go to buy a car you will be on your guard, because you know that salesmen have to sell cars to make a living. You are under no illusions; you know you may be fortunate to get out of the showroom without surrendering your telephone number, and the permission to give you a follow-up call.

If you do not buy the car, you will receive phone calls from a sales team heralding great deals and special offers until you do make a purchase. The only way out is to tell them you have bought something else, have recently been made bankrupt, or that the army is sending you to Afghanistan for a year. In the latter case, you will probably be told there is a discount for troops going to war.

A second scenario might involve you walking into a bank to ask for some investment advice. Most people just do not understand what they are walking into. The fact is that you are walking into a sales franchise just like Ford, Nissan, Mercedes, or BMW. In this case, the franchise is the Post Office, Lloyds, Barclays, HSBC, Royal Bank of Scotland, or the local building society.

Comparing the terminology

Glossary	Car sales	Banking
Premises	Showroom	Branch
Personnel	Sales manager	Customer adviser, investment adviser, investment consultant, business adviser, branch manager, customer liaison officer
Business	Brand Franchise	Banking Group
Services offered	Car sales and servicing	Investment sales
Cost of advice	Commission is built into the cost price	Free advice, but a lump sum charge at the point of sale.
Source of profit	Percentage of car sale price	Percentage of investment sale
	Car servicing fees	Annual charges on the investment

Your local bank is a sales outlet

> "What is the difference between buying from a car salesman and the advice from your bank? – There is no difference except you understand the rules when you buy a new car"

Banks are smart when it comes to selling. The sales people are called customer advisers, investment advisers, investment consultants, business advisers, branch managers, and customer liaison officers. There is no mention of selling but their earnings are linked to sales commissions. They have targets, and this is why the counter staff harasses you for unrelated products when all you want to do is pay the water bill. No bank customer adviser is ever going to tell you there are better deals with another bank.

Everyone in the industry knows that the in-house bank advisers will go through a list of all the current accounts with a healthy balance, then phone all such account holders one by one and say, "we should review your finances" which is really meaning they wish to sell you a stock market investment or an Investment Bond.

If you thought you were going to get straight and honest investment advice from a bank you are going to be very disappointed.

You may need to think about this statement for a moment, but I have never come across anyone who has become bankrupt without a lot of debt. I have been in this industry, investing, for over 30 years and the people who get into trouble are those who have too much debt. Debt has its place – to help you build a business and buy a house, but do not fall in love with it because it will not fall in love with you. In fact, if you use debt to buy things that you do not really need, as soon as your financial resilience is tested you are going to have to sell the things you really do need. So getting rid of debt can be a very good idea.

Now, let's suppose a family with a mortgage of £200,000 has a stroke of luck. A distant relative who they never met just died, and they inherit £200,000. They are delighted to have the windfall but soon worry because they haven't a clue what to do next, so they go to the bank to ask for advice.

What should the bank advise? Paying off the mortgage could be a very good option, and with no debt the family can save the money that would have been the monthly mortgage repayments. Without any risk in this decision, they could be on the road to financial independence.

But no, the bank's 'investment adviser' says, "Keep the mortgage and buy some investments that can help to make you richer". The investment risks are understated in the impressive literature, and the costs of investing not at all clear. We already know the family does not understand the first thing about investing and it is vulnerable to sales talk masquerading as investment advice.

Had this poor advice been given to the family just before the credit crunch, or just before the bursting of the tech bubble, a lot of the inherited money would have been lost – typically between £30,000 and £60,000. The mortgage would still be £200,000 and there would not be enough money left to repay it. But the bank is happy because it keeps a profitable mortgage customer who continues to pay interest on the £200,000 mortgage. Also, the bank adviser has earned a very good bonus that month with £6,000 to £12,000 commission earned and the bank continues to earn a fee every year from the investment management.

Let us look at the details from the bank's perspective. If the bank had given the right advice to the family, there would be no customer. There would be no mortgage as this would be paid off, no money to buy investments and there would be no commission for the sales staff.

In defence of the banks' sales staff, in my opinion, most of them do not know much about investing either, and their limited training is geared to selling the bank's own investment products.[10]

If the family had been prepared to pay a fee for professional advice, either on an hourly rate or a fixed fee, they could have received fair advice. The problem is that we all love a bargain, and we are lured in by the magnetic idea of getting free advice. Unfortunately, when a customer buys an investment based on free advice, it usually turns out to be the most expensive option.

Do not be in any doubt. If you are being offered free advice, then you are sleepwalking into a sales process. I appreciate that in the modern world you can get a little free advice. It may be on a website, or through a seminar, but no one is going to spend hours giving you free advice without there being a good chance of a substantial commission.

Unfortunately, many people do not understand this concept at all. They just do not want to pay a fee, despite it being absolutely essential to receive good advice when planning for the future. In our story the family ends up keeping a mortgage when it would have been so much better off without one. They may also have been sold a high-risk investment portfolio, which could end up losing them money.

Since the credit crunch and the obvious failure of banks to manage their own affairs, more of us are looking for an alternative source of advice, although many would-be investors still think the banks are a good option.

---

10 NatWest Bank trained 1,000 advisers for its 'Money Sense' campaign, which started in 2008. Advisers are said to have had an average of only eight hours bespoke training to provide free 'impartial advice' in its branches. A cynic might ask if the £4 million cost to the bank was enough to guarantee high quality advice to customers. Source: Citywire 11.12.2008

Commissions

In my entire career spanning over 30 years I have not encountered a single person with a mortgage who, upon taking advice from a commission-based adviser, was encouraged to repay it when they had the means to do so. In the same way that a car salesman will never recommend a bicycle as a prudent alternative, a commission-based financial adviser is unlikely to recommend anything that will leave him with no commission.

This 'legalised theft' has been concealed in the past by a booming stock market, until the dotcom bubble burst. Only high stock market returns could cover the high charges being levied by advisers and fund managers. In recent times the ability to conceal these high investment charges has gone.

The headlines following the credit crunch focused on Government interventions to rescue failing banks, and the massive national debt we now have as a result. During all of this the plight of the private investor has been overlooked.

The conflict of commission v good advice

I have criticised banks and fund managers as bastions of poor investment advice, but I do not wish to be unfair and fail to mention the same criticism applies to any advice from those who earn a living through commissions.

To be absolutely clear, I should point out the obvious fact that those who work in investment sales – and car sales – are not all horrible and dishonest people. But they are in a job where the culture *necessarily* revolves entirely around selling, because the only way they can make a living is to sell.

The best hook they have is the offer of free advice. Do not

fall for it! There is no such thing as free advice, other than access to an online planning tool or a simple piece of advice to give you a flavour of a service being offered to you.

If you fall for the lure of free advice, you are being pulled into the world of investment sales, not investment advice.

Independent financial advice

At the time of writing, the FSA's proposal[11] is that all independent advice should be fee-based from 2012 and advisers must have a much higher level of professional qualifications.

There is still time for investors to be paying through the nose for free advice, and investors will need to be on their guard, as the big institutions have always managed to sidestep the interests of the consumer. There will always be those who look to swindle us within the limits of the law.

---

11 The Conservative party has stated it intends to abolish the FSA so the proposals may not come to pass. Also, EU legislation may override the UK Government's proposals.

Would you lose your home in a fire?

"The real scam is the risk of taking advice."
—Financial Times, February 2009

IMAGINE YOU are having a conversation with your friends, a married couple in their mid 30's, and you consider them to be good at managing their money. You often have enlightening conversations with them – they do good research, and they share their findings. They save you money on household bills and shopping, and you learn which cars are the most reliable and economical.

One day, they grab your interest with news of how to save yourself a few hundred pounds a year. They say, "We have decided not to bother insuring our house." The new house they bought at a bargain price during a housing slump is built with all the modern safety features available. It complies with all new fire regulations, and has a modern failsafe electrical system. They tell you that the chance of their house burning down is negligible. In their locality they have never heard of a house flooding or of one being struck by lightning. When you pay your house insurance, they say, insurance companies just pocket your premiums.

Would you think this was sensible? Would you follow this advice? I think most people would decide that this is a risk not worth taking. If your house did burn down, or was struck by lightning or flooded, this would be a terrible blow and it would be a point of ruin for most of us.

Three years pass, then five years, and there have been no fires, or lightning strikes, or floods, and by now they've saved a lot by not paying an insurance premium. They may even point a finger and say, "We told you so!" You then find out that all of your friends have stopped insuring their homes and this is the tipping point when I expect that even the most sensible people might follow what everyone else is doing. There is a collective denial that the risk is not that much of a risk after all.

Of course, I hope and expect, you will not be influenced by reading about this money saving idea, and you will continue to insure your home. The consequences of an uninsured fire or a storm would be unthinkable.

It is one thing not to insure your mobile phone or your camera, because losing one of these is not going to postpone your retirement or destroy your financial life. Not insuring your home is a very high-risk strategy.

There is no doubt that people get away with silly risks. You might enjoy the thrill of putting your hand in the lion's cage on a visit to the zoo and go home with both arms still attached to the rest of your body, but this does not make it a good idea. We must weigh up the benefit of an action with the potential consequences.

However, there is a weakness in the way we interpret risk. The fact is that not many of us have suffered the total loss of our house burning down or that of being struck by lightning. We generally call on all our life experiences when making a decision, hence the saying 'once bitten twice shy', but if you have not had a personal experience, it is difficult to assess the magnitude of the risk relative to the benefits.

When the Romans built their homes on the very fertile slopes of Mount Vesuvius, no one in living memory had experienced a volcano eruption, a once in every 1,000 year disaster.

In recent years in England, too many people have bought new homes that have been built on what used to be called floodplains. In the past these low-lying flat areas were left undeveloped for a reason. Once every few generations, people expected higher than average rainfall, and the fields would transform into lakes. During the greed of the property boom planners and developers ignored such wisdom.

So were the buyers foolish not to have checked out the fact their new homes were not built on firm foundations, or was it the fault of the developers and the other professionals involved? I side with the buyer, because it would have been reasonable to expect the properties to have been built with a minimum degree of care.

The problem is that those involved in the profit making process of building new homes were all wearing their short-term hats. The buyers, at the other end of the timescale, were looking at a long-term commitment. If something such as a flood has not happened for a generation or two, it can easily be forgotten. However, a cursory glance at the records would have shown that these houses are likely to be flooded at least once every 50 years.

This kind of negligent short sightedness regularly occurs in the world of investment advice.

The industry's wealth destroying behaviour

When taking professional advice, we are told the value of investments can go down as well as up, but usually the risk is not quantified. We may be advised there will be good years and some poor years. Different people will have a different perception of what a poor year is, but not many would anticipate a total collapse of their investments.

Any investment professional should know to expect the financial world's equivalent of a flood or a volcano erupting at regular intervals. During our lifetime of investing we should expect three or four periods of crisis but we cannot predict when or in what form they will arrive. It is also impossible to predict the magnitude of the consequences.

During good times there will be long periods of high profits for investors holding property, stock market funds and high yielding bonds but it is certain that these investments will also be hit, sometimes for long periods, by a wealth-destroying crisis.

Regretfully, most professionals do not incorporate catastrophe risk into their investment strategies. It is one thing for the banks and insurance companies to mismanage their own businesses, and quite another to let down their customers. Think of it as an adventurer attempting to climb an almost impossible cliff face without a rope. It is his choice to put himself in danger, but quite another to lead a party of students up the precipice with him.

Far too many people have suffered because their investment portfolios had no insurance for the financial storms when they came, and the following chart shows they come frequently.[12]

Like the people who do not insure their home, a flawed idea can seem to work well for years, but then the investors have to watch their investments burn. Unlike houses, financial

---

12 At the time of writing the credit crunch outcome is not known, but it seems not to be on the scale of the early 1970's bear market when the stock market fell 66% and lasted over 20 years.

WOULD YOU LOSE YOUR HOME IN A FIRE?

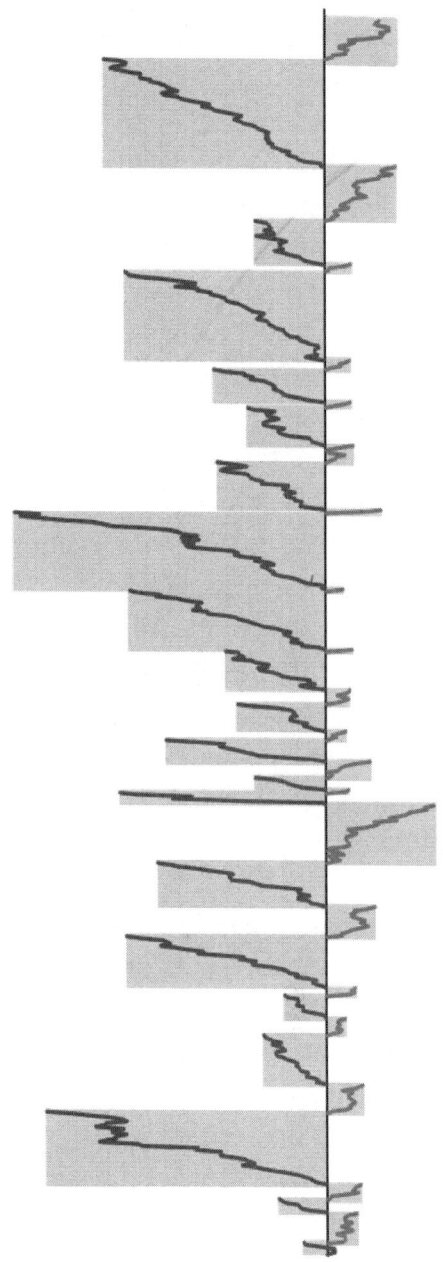

Chart to show the frequency of Bull and Bear Markets
Based on the FTSE All-Share Index from 1955 to 2009

The average duration of a bull market 23 months
the average duration of a bear market 10 months

markets always get burned at some time, so protection should be an essential part of investment planning.

Why would an insurance company, a bank, or an IFA leave customers exposed to regular events that could be catastrophic? It could be ignorance, it could be short-term thinking applied to a long-term problem, or it could be because advisers are dependent on commission income. It could also be simply because a number of investment companies have ignored the catastrophe risk, and the rest all begin to copy them to save on costs. In the end, they all burn together.

When there is a catastrophe, it is the investor's capital that is lost. It is not usually the investment manager's money or the adviser's money. Investors unknowingly carry the big risk.

You cannot avoid losses during a crisis, but you can certainly design a portfolio to limit the damage so you are in a position to recover and get back on track.

The insurance I am talking about is not paid as a premium to an insurance company, but it takes the form of choosing a number of investments that have genuine defensive qualities during a downturn. These are the investments to carry you through a crisis, but when times are good they can look boring.

During the good times the defensive investments do not make much money compared to the best performing stock market investments. So they have a cost, or a price, which is simply that of making less profit during the good times.

When memories are short, and the professionals forget about the last crisis, or they have no knowledge of the dangers, these defensive investments are overlooked.

Most adults, if they start investing at a young age, have a chance to invest for 50 years or longer. If they do not build their portfolios to withstand a financial crisis they are going to have three, four, or five chances of suffering a disaster. The reason so few of us fail to protect our portfolios is because the industry encourages us to take a short-term view.

It would be ridiculous to say we could have forecast the consequences of the credit crunch or the dotcom bubble, but it is good practice to allow for future disasters when we invest. No one will escape from a future crisis, but the smart investor will survive, and be able to view it as a temporary setback.

Institutional memory loss

In recent years the finance industry has suffered the result of a particularly severe case of short-term memory loss. It disregarded completely the history of investing, which cautions that we must always be prepared for a downturn.

The consequence of being totally unprepared for a crisis is that during the 'technology bubble' many insurance companies were brought to the brink of collapse, and the FSA forced insurers to change their investment strategies to avoid the risk of a failed industry. It is thought that the last big downturn of the UK stock market in early 2003 was the result of the forced selling of stock market assets by insurance companies, somewhat like a 'fire sale' driving down the price of stocks.

As it turned out, the FSA's action was too late for many insurance companies, the damage was already done, and they were left in such a weak position that many did not have the financial strength to continue independently. Many of them are now either closed to new business or merged with other insurers. Friends Provident, London Life, Scottish Mutual, Scottish Amicable, NPI, Scottish Equitable, Clerical

Medical and Scottish Widows have all either lost their independence or closed.

Of course, the real casualties are not the institutions but the customers who invested and were rewarded with big losses or poor investment returns.

The not so perfect investments

"The reason we hold truth in such respect is because we have so little opportunity to get familiar with it."

—Mark Twain's notebook 1898.

INTEREST RATES are now much lower than they have been in the past, so there are many investors who need more income to make ends meet. However, many of them do not like the volatility that comes with stock market investing, and the risk of losses. If experts could put together a packaged investment that offered them a high income, and the advantage of high stock market returns without the risk, this would represent the 'Holy Grail' of investing.

This has created an industry that purports to design perfect investment products where you can have your cake and eat it.

You can buy an investment with a rate of 8% after tax, for example, and have your money back after 5 years. This is more than double the rate of interest available from the best bank accounts at the time of writing.

When presented with such an investment opportunity, a number of questions should immediately spring to mind. How can I get such a high return with the absence of any risk? How is this investment immune to market fluctuations?

If it really is such an amazing investment, how has it been kept a secret from the rest of the world for so long?

Think of the magician performing a trick. You know it is sleight of the hand, but as hard as you look you cannot work it out. Often, the trick rests on the misdirection of the magician – at the key moment, you will be looking in the wrong place. If you do happen to look in the right direction, you can often spot the deception.

In the same way, these amazing investment products may distract your attention with the promise of high returns and low risk. All will seem well, until the next financial storm exposes their very non-magical, fragile nature.

Some investors have benefited from compensation,[13] when poor advice could be proved, but often the investor takes the full loss because the risk warnings were in the documents. The marketing literature does contain a warning that the investor's capital is not secure but we often rely on what is said during the sales meeting. The warnings in the product literature can be undermined by verbal assurances that the risks are minimal.

The industry essentially adheres to the following axioms when selling us this kind of investment:

- Mindless optimism is the best approach.
- This seems to work most of the time.

When everything in the world is fine, the risks inherent in the packaged investment products sold by banks, insurance companies and advisers are not obvious at all, unless you

---

13 In 2009 the Financial Services Ombudsman said it had dealt with an increased number of complaints relating to banks advising clients to buy inappropriate high-risk investments.

are an educated professional. Even then, the nature of the risk often cannot be quantified.

These investments have lost investors billions of pounds but they continue to be a lucrative source of income for the fund managers and advisers. Investors do not understand the risks they are taking, often because the advisers do not understand them either.

I say these investments are toxic, because they can expose investors to serious losses or poor investment returns. The most common toxic investments are covered in the appendix. It is worth familiarising yourself with them, as you should avoid them like the plague. Investors holding one or more of these investments should consider the ways to manage an exit.

The outrageous cost of investing

"....it cannot be right to hide the cost of advice from consumers.... A paradigm shift is needed."
—Dan Waters, FSA Director of Retail Policy.

ECONOMISTS MUST struggle when they study the selling tactics of financial products. In a market with hundreds of different traders all selling a similar product, you would expect that competition would drive down costs and prices. This rarely happens in the world of investing.

When car manufacturers are fighting for customers we see new models with lower prices and more extras fitted as standard. Furniture outlets halve their prices, and supermarkets encourage trade with 'buy one, get one free' offers. However, encouraging new investors with good value for money has never caught on in Britain.

I believe that most people *do* try to find the better deal, but quickly discover that this is not as straightforward as shopping for food or furniture. There are so many ways for the actual cost to be obscured that people feel none the wiser after a genuine attempt at researching the best product for their circumstances. Many end up investing with the last salesperson they meet, or the first one to give them a follow-up call. We are always met with the same pattern – past performance figures, some financial jargon, and then an attempt to close a sale. If all of the most obvious sources of advice take this approach, then what can you do?

Perhaps management fees stay as high as they do because investments and pensions are sold, rather than bought. Investors are lured in by a sophisticated, target-driven sales system. At the end of the day, this system needs to be paid for.

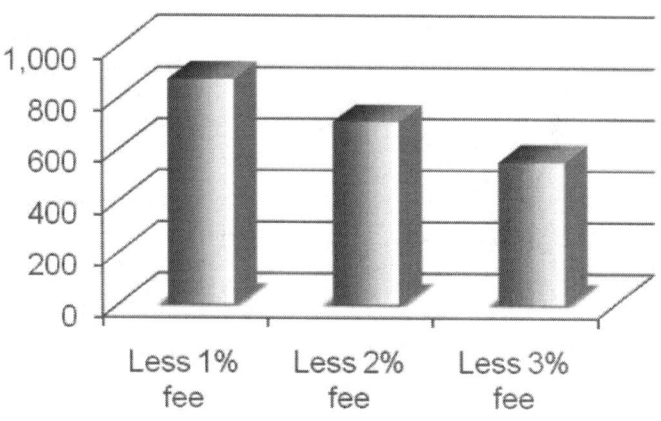

Fees do matter

According to one of the main research organisations, annual management fees have gone up from 1.3% in 1994 to 1.6% in 2008. It may not sound a lot, but when you add more cost to something that is already too expensive, year after year, it begins to have a significant effect on the investment returns. In America, where individuals are more likely to make their own buying decisions, the cost of investing has reduced in recent years.

Commission and the lure of free advice

THE LURE of free advice is very strong. Perhaps people expect free advice for investing because we do not expect to pay a fee to save money in a deposit account.[14]

We understand a bank will pay us interest on a deposit account and then lend it to someone else charging a higher rate, as this is how the banks makes a profit. There is no direct cost to us.

Investing is totally different. The banks, insurance companies and sales people know that if they continue to recommend commission paying products, rather than charging a fee for advice, they will have a profitable existence.

A potential customer is known in the business as 'a prospect'. Let us assume a salesman working for a bank speaks to ten potential customers seeking advice in a day. If he only manages to complete a sale with five of them, this more than compensates for the other five who could not be persuaded

---

14 Investors do need to be careful when taking advice about deposit accounts from a commission-earning financial adviser. The investor may end up with a lower interest rate than they should – in order to attract deposits, a growing number of banks and building societies will pay an adviser a commission that is deducted from the customer's interest.

to take the bait. The commission made on the sales is more than enough to pay for all the 'wasted time'.

I meet people on a regular basis who believe they have had free advice, because they did not get a bill in the post. The reality is that they did pay for the advice, and the cost was taken directly from their investment.

How much commission are we talking about?

Typically, an Investment Bond will earn 5% commission on a sale. Invest £10,000 and there is £500 commission for an adviser. Invest £100,000 and there is £5,000 commission. Billions of pounds worth of bonds have been sold, collectively earning commission-based sellers a handsome profit. In addition to the initial fee, there is often an ongoing commission of 0.5% a year, so an adviser can build up a stream of income from past sales, often for doing nothing.

The difference made by a commission charge		
£100,000 invested at 6%	5 years	10 years
No initial charge	£133,822	£179,084
6% initial charge	£125,793	£168,339
The difference	£8,029	£10,745

In the table above, the initial charge has effectively resulted in a year of no profit. This cost drags down the investment return forever.

High costs, often due to scandalous levels of commission, are found in many investment products including personal pensions and ISAs. Advisers typically receive commissions of 3% or 4%, often 5% and up to 8% plus 0.5% ongoing commission a year.

It is important to remember that this commission does not come out of some sort of marketing allowance. Any commission paid to an adviser will be deducted directly from your savings.

Discounts

Often, the commission to an adviser will be higher, if it is expected that an IFA firm will be able to produce a lot of business for the fund manager or insurance company.

This allows attractive sales campaigns, which offer a discount if you invest 'this month'. If investment advisers have a high profit margin and a good database of existing clients, it is not difficult to offer a 1%, 2%, or 3% discount and have a profitable campaign.

Occasionally, there are discounts representing 5%, which are close to giving up most of the initial commission, and the long-term profit comes from all those accumulating 0.5%'s.

If you can secure a discount during one of these campaigns, this will reduce the cost, but do not be lulled into thinking you have bought a cheap investment during the sale of the century.

Special allocations

As a child I always thought it was unfair to be given something by someone, and then later to be asked to give it back. Insurance companies regularly pull this kind of trick.

You buy an investment and you are given a 'special allocation', or welcoming present, of 5% or 8%. You have invested £100,000 and your first statement indicates a worth of £108,000. However, if you need to cash in a year later, the penalty may well be 9%. The policy conditions show the scale of penalties in the first five, or seven years, but your attention was likely drawn away from this penalty clause by the 'special allocation.'

This is a little like buying 11 slices of bacon for the price of 10, then getting home to find the packet only contains 9 slices because you opened it too early.

The penalty for having your own money back exists to pay for the commission to the adviser. It is also common for the annual charges to be higher in the first five years or so, to cover the high setting up cost. The table below shows how this type of charging might work out.

What a difference a special allocation can make		
	5 years	10 years
No special allocation* £100,000 invested at 6%	£130,696	£170,814
6% special allocation** £106,000 invested at 6%	£122,883	£153,134
The extra cost of a special allocation	£7,813	£17,680

*0.5% annual charge for a low cost plan. **Extra 1.5% p.a. charge for the first 5 years; 1.5% normal annual charge thereafter.

How to guarantee you beat the average investor

Investment returns are uncertain because we do not know how stock markets, bonds or interest rates will perform in the future. However, before investing we should know how much it costs to invest, as this will have a direct effect on the profits.

If one bank offered you an interest rate of 3%, and a second bank offered you 5%, if all the conditions of the account were the same you would take the 5%. If you invest £100,000 this would make an extra £2,000 a year. It is not a difficult choice to make.

If I met someone who had a bank account with an interest rate of 3%, and they could not be bothered to sign a form to earn 5%, I would ask if I could sign the form for them and then split the extra £2,000 between us every year. Put this way, most people would probably decide to sign the form themselves after all.

It is no different when buying an investment or pension contract. That extra charge of 1% or 2% a year makes exactly the same difference, and it has a huge impact over time.

When you invest there are always two main sets of charges to consider. The first is the initial charge or setting up cost, and the second is the annual cost or management charge.

Commission is only one part of the equation, it is an important part, but it is more important to know the total costs.[15]

You should aim to pay a maximum of 1% a year for a fund and a set up fee of no more than 1%. The good news is that in recent times such low costs have become a realistic target.

---

15   See the appendix for a discussion about costs.

A summary of the bad practices that cost you money

If I had to live my life again, I'd make the same mistakes, only sooner
—Tallulah Bankhead

THIS FIRST section is designed to put you on your guard and to protect you from the sales tactics of the industry. Keep the following points in mind at all times:

- A common tactic is to confuse you with marketing material masquerading as educational material.
- Be sceptical when you are shown past performance figures – they are often manipulated. Past performance is no indication of future performance and there is no academic evidence to support this myth.
- There are very few who can consistently out-perform the market averages and it is impossible to identify them in advance. Avoid 'star' fund managers.
- Do not base any decisions on forecasting, as there is no evidence to show it has any value.
- The majority of advisers, banks and insurance companies are out-and-out sales operations. The free advice on offer should be declined as it only leads to expensive investment products.

- If an investment seems too good to be true, it is too good to be true. Many of the investments sold in packages appear to offer high returns and little risk. Generally the return potential is overstated and the risk is understated.
- It is good practice to be prepared for future disasters when planning your investments. Disasters often start with an optimistic promise to outperform.

SECTION 2
PLANNING AND UNDERSTANDING THE RISKS

Avoiding death on the operating table – have a plan

MEDICINE HAS made great advances in recent times, but these advances are sometimes initially sensationalised. We often see exciting reports of new treatments, but when we browse past the headlines it becomes apparent that any cure is years away.

I was therefore intrigued when I read of a breakthrough in medicine that immediately resulted in a dramatic drop in the number of deaths and complications following surgery.[1] Overnight, the rate of surgical complications fell by more than one-third and inpatient deaths fell by over 40%.

This major advance came down to the use of a simple checklist. It may seem remarkable that a 19-item surgical safety checklist, designed to improve team communication and consistency of care, could have such an effect. But it did.

Bearing this in mind, you should not underestimate the importance of writing down your financial plan in an ordered fashion. This will dramatically improve the chances of achieving your financial goals in life.

1 The study was led by the World Health Organisation: New England Journal of Medicine publication of January 2009

The start of the plan can be a summary of your short and long-term goals, and your ambitions for you and your family. Once you have these out of your head and onto paper, you can investigate how achievable they are relative to what you are doing now.

A written plan helps you on your financial journey in exactly the same way as a road map helps you to get from A to B. If you do not plan your journey it is likely it is going to end up being more expensive because you are certain to miss the best route.

In-depth planning is beyond the scope of this book. However, you will need to have a good understanding of the action you must take to face the future successfully and to have the chance of achieving your financial goals in life.

Specifics that should be understood are the effects of an increasing expectation of life, the risks of investing relative to living a long life and the corrosive effect of inflation. The diagrams below show how you could start your plan.

If you do not map your financial destination you will still arrive somewhere, but it is unlikely it will be where you want to be.

Long and short-term goals

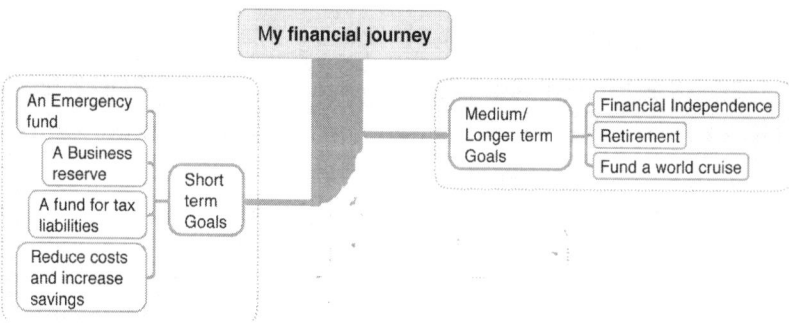

Building up your plan

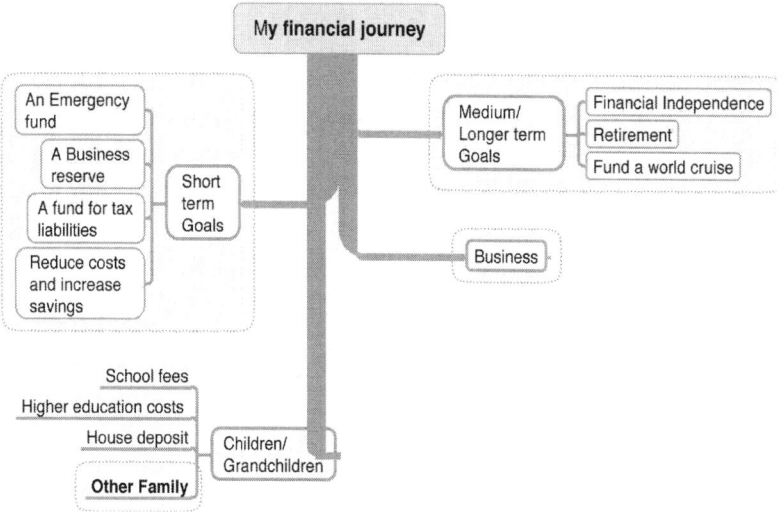

Living to the age of 100

"I'll say that there will come a time when being old is cooler than being young, because what being old will represent is power. It will represent money. It will represent having survived. It will represent wisdom."

—*Freakonomics* author, Stephen Dubner

IF YOU ever think about assessing your life expectancy, it is likely you will underestimate how long you will live.

Typical excuses for not planning our long term future often run along the lines of "everyone in my family dies young", or "a friend of a friend died two weeks after his retirement". There is also the ever popular "you might get run over by a bus tomorrow." Whilst an early death is possible, fatalistic viewpoints such as these are blind to the reality of an ageing population. Between 1900 and the year 2000, the average life expectancy increased by 25 years. So, in a manner of speaking, people lived 3 months longer for every year that passed.

Only 1 in 4 males born in 1901 could expect to live until retirement, and even then they would survive retirement for less than a year. In the 1940's, the average payout length of the State Pension scheme was less than 3 years.

The situation now could hardly be more different, and the prospect of a long retirement is a likely one. 9 out of 10 now make it to the State retirement age, and as our life expectancy continues to improve, the shape of society is changing.

Scientists have said the life span for a human being may be much longer than most of us have previously thought possible. Steven Austad, of the University Of Texas Health Science Center, has said that he is certain that some children alive now will live to be 150.

The problem that comes with the good fortune of a longer life is that the investment pot now needs to be bigger, or it will not last long enough. 50 years ago, if you lived to the age of 70 you would be complimented for 'a good innings'. Nowadays, this is no longer an impressive feat.

It is easy to forget the huge medical advances that have taken place. It seems amazing that it was only in 1953 that a doctor published a paper that established the link between exercise and the prevention of heart attacks. Before this it was thought that exercise was only good for the soul. When the paper was published, it was generally received with disbelief by the medical profession.[2]

Now, when we prepare for our retirement years it seems perfectly reasonable to assume that we may live to the age of 100. When we think about living so long it can make previous ideas about money redundant. The chances of inheriting a life-changing sum from parents are now more remote, as their nest egg will now provide for a long retirement. As parents live longer, their children may be well into their middle ages by the time they receive what is left.

Any potential inheritance may be further diminished if a parent's savings have been used to provide for the heavy cost

---

2 'Coronary heart-disease and physical activity at work' by Dr Jerry Morris: published in The Lancet in 1953.

of medical care in the final years. From a parent's perspective, there is a need to plan well if there is an intention to provide for the next generation and grandchildren.

If we are to be scientific about life expectancy we should know that most insurers base their life expectancy calculations on something called the 1992 Cohort series. This is a benchmark based on actuarial experience of mortality in 1992.

The tables were revised in 1999 due to a sudden increase in life expectancy beyond 65. Many assumed at the time this sudden increase was a one-off event and would not be repeated, but it soon became apparent that life expectancy will continue to rise.

Is it realistic to retire at 50, 55, or 60 if you can look forward to 40 or 50 years of retirement, active and in relatively good health? How would you fund your retirement without dropping your living standards?

The State Pension

When the State Pension improved, following World War II, it provided a valuable benefit. It did not cost the Government very much as most of the population died before retirement age, and the rest only lived long enough to enjoy two or three years of leisure.

The cost of the State pension is now a major item of Government expenditure, as the great majority of us will receive a pension and expect to receive it for a long time.

Moving the retirement age for women to age 65 was the first step to reduce the cost of the State Pension. However, even if the State pension age gradually moves to age 70, it will be necessary for future Governments to somehow put a cap on the costs of pensions and other State benefits.

As the retired increase in number and the workforce reduces, the cost of pensions could be crippling for Government finances. An ageing population will also put pressure on the NHS, and social services. The system must help the needy, and yet be affordable.

Many believe that there will have to be an extension of means testing, when only those without private pensions or savings will receive a State pension, and only the poor will get financial help from the State.

At the moment those who are retired have a minimum income guarantee every week, so those who have not saved receive more State help than those who have savings. The present tax and benefit system seems to discourage savings, but the huge national debt should change Government policy. With a growing retired population, future governments may have to settle for a State system that provides only enough to keep those in need off the breadline.

It is certain that state retirement benefits are not going to get any better. We must decide if we are prepared to rely on a future Government improving retirement support or if we should carefully plan for our own self-sufficiency.

Annuities

An increase in life expectancy has tremendous importance to those thinking about buying an annuity.[3] For example,

---

3 An annuity is the exchange of a lump sum for a guaranteed income for life. When a private pension fund is used to buy an annuity contract with an insurance company a longer life expectation reduces the amount of the annual pension income.

outstanding annuity policies in the UK total an estimated £100 billion and adding just one additional year of life expectancy requires insurance companies to add £3.5 billion to their reserves.

Final salary company pension schemes are disappearing due to the increasingly high cost of providing them to employees. More workers will have to have their own personal pension plans, and be responsible for their own investment decisions.

For the personal pension saver, a pension fund only buys half the annuity it used to 20 years ago. For a given level of income the pension pot needs to be twice as big as it used to, because the annuity income will have to be paid out for many more years than in the past.

How long might you live?

You should assume you are going to live for a long time, because the alternative is using up all your money in your early dotage, and then not being able to do anything about it. The only sensible option is to assume you are going to be around for quite a while.[4]

No one knows how long the improvement in life expectancy can continue. We are often told the younger generation, due to their sedentary lifestyle and poor eating habits, may

---

4 It is interesting to note that expectation of life in Kensington and Chelsea is about 10 years longer than in Manchester. This is connected to the local population's standard of living. It would be reasonable to expect those reading this book to have a higher expectation of life than the general population, as your standard of living will be higher than the average UK citizen!

have a shorter life expectancy than the previous generation. On the other hand, the maximum life span for a human being may be longer than most of us imagine.

There must be a limit to the extent that medical science can prolong life, and limited investment in the NHS combined with an ageing population will mean that prolonging life at all costs will no longer be affordable for everyone.

Only those with a budget to pay for advanced treatments will be able to benefit from them. Advanced dental treatment, such as implants and other orthodontic work, is not available on the NHS. As pressure on the NHS budget increases, other treatments may also only be available to private patients.

Inflation – we should change our perception of risk

> *By a continuing process of inflation, government can confiscate, secretly and unobserved, an important part of the wealth of their citizens*
>
> —John Maynard Keynes

IMAGINE TAKING a walk in the countryside, and accidentally wandering into a field occupied by a large bull. Most people would leave this field very quickly, and would be quite happy to take an alternative route through a field occupied by a herd of cows. Bulls, of course, are very dangerous animals, and are not to be trifled with.

In practice, however, cows inflict much more damage on the general public than bulls, particularly when their young are in the herd. Cows usually kill a few ramblers every year, and many more are seriously injured. Cows also kill agricultural workers and hundreds of them are injured in serious accidents.

Obviously, bulls do kill and injure people, but we take action to avoid bulls. It is obvious from their appearance that they are dangerous. Statistically, however, more people are gored or crushed to death when they walk through a field of cows. A cow, of course, weighs close to a ton. The matriarch of the herd, scared that ramblers will hurt their young, will often lead a phalanx of cattle to charge and crush them.

In practice, there is no need to stay at home in the city for fear of a cow-related death. Once you take the time to understand the dangers, you can safely enjoy the benefits of a relaxing countryside stroll. In any case, according to accident and emergency statistics staying at home is a hazardous affair – particularly if you scale a ladder, or enjoy a spot of DIY. And, you are more likely to be run over by a car than a cow.

Like the rambler who strolls amongst cows, most investors have comparable misconceptions about what can be dangerous. The commonly overlooked hazard when planning for a long life is inflation.

7% is a big number

When the financial press speculates on future growth, we routinely see figures of around 7% being thrown around. Such is the casual use of 7% in growth forecasts, you might have come to regard the number as something that should not be a concern.

Nothing could be further from the truth. It is important that you understand this, so I'm going to use some simple mathematics to illustrate just how important 7% can be.

The term 'exponential function' is used to describe the growth of something that is expected to grow steadily. If I start by saying that a tree will grow by 7% a year, we could plot the exponential function on a graph. The graph would clearly show the rate at which the tree will grow by the fixed amount of 7% every year. The tree will take a year to grow

7% taller, but it will take a longer length of time to double in height – what we would call the 'doubling time'.

There is an easy way of working out the doubling time. You simply divide the number 70 (see footnote 5) and in this example we divide it by 7. This leaves us with 10. So it takes the tree 10 years to double in height. If it is 50 feet tall now, it will be 100 feet tall in 10 years and a massive 200 feet in 20 years. This is important because I often see the number 7 used in growth projections.

The population of the town in which I live has increased from 5,000 to 20,000 in the last 30 years. If someone said the town was now growing at a rate of 7% a year you would struggle to get the local newspaper to show any interest. But if you told the editor the population would grow to be 160,000 in 30 years time, people will begin to pay attention because the whole character of the place is going to change.

There is another consequence of this arithmetic. If you take 70 years as a period of time, and note that that this used to be regarded as one human lifetime, three score years and ten, 7% inflation over 70 years gives you a 128 fold increase in prices. In the modern world, our expectation of life is approaching the age of 90 and we could regard 70 years as being our adult life expectation.[6]

There have been long periods in the past when inflation

---

5 The number 70 is approximately 100 multiplied by the natural logarithm of two. Mathematically speaking it is logical but all you need to understand is the number 70.

6 There is a very important observation here, which is that the last doubling time is greater than all the preceding growth. For example, when we go from a 64-fold increase to 128-fold increase in prices, the additional increase in prices is larger than all of the previous price increases put together.

ran at the rate of 7%[7] and there is no reason to say we will experience long periods of 7% inflation in the future. In living memory inflation has ranged from 0.7% to 24.9% a year, so 7% is nowhere near the top or the bottom of the range.

So now we can begin to understand that what might seem a harmless number can present us with a significant problem as we grow older and live longer than we used to. Living longer should be good news, as long as we can afford to live.

For someone about to hit retirement age, it would be reasonable to anticipate prices increasing eight-fold, or sixteen-fold without the need to be optimistic about their chances of a long life – and they avoid cigarettes, take some exercise and have three portions of vegetables a day.

If you are unhappy because a litre of petrol is over £1 and a pint of lager is often £4, these could increase to a wallet melting £16 and £64 if inflation is 7% during your retirement.[8] If your time horizon is 50 years, the cost of some everyday goods will have so many zeros that you may confuse the price with your phone number.

---

7 In the 40-year period from 1950 to 1990, inflation ran at the average rate of 7%. Also, in the 25 years from 1970 to 2005 inflation ran at the average rate of 7%.
8 In the 40 years to the end of 2008 the cost of beer and petrol has increased 15 fold: very close to an average of 7% a year.

Investing for a millionaire lifestyle – 1980 to 2008

THE ADVERTS for lottery tickets like to offer us the chance of an instant million, but a million will not do what it used to do in 'the good old days'. Going back to 1980, when we were only four years away from George Orwell's '1984', a million pounds deposited in a building society account paid 10.5% net of basic rate tax, so the interest of £105,000 a year was enough to support what we would then call a millionaire's lifestyle.

Unfortunately, this high income was an illusion. Inflation was over 15% in 1980, down from over 17% the year before. The truth was that an interest rate of 10.5% was well below the level needed to keep up with rising prices. Leaving all of the interest to accumulate would not have been enough to satisfy the relentless appetite of inflation.

However, if you stuck your head in the sand when the subject of inflation came up, as most people did, a building society investment seemed fantastic.

In 1980 savers actually needed an after tax return of 15%, the sort of experience you only normally get in a banana republic or Zimbabwe, because the value of the money in your pocket seems to fall faster than you can spend it, when inflation is so high.

Fast forward to 2008, and with inflation running at under 1%, it seemed to be less of a problem. For the no-risk investor requiring an income, bank deposits could pay 4% net of tax. But all is not well for our millionaire investor. The £105,000 income has dropped to £40,000 after-tax, and since 1980, inflation has more than tripled the price of everything.[9]

By 2009, investors were doing very well if they could find an account paying 4% net of tax, so those relying on interest to make ends meet saw their standard of living collapse. As an investment philosophy, the exclusive use of deposit accounts for long-term savings is badly flawed.

In the short-term, drawing interest can seem ideal, but the purchasing power of the investment will quietly slip away over time. The £1 million of capital will remain, but it will not buy as much as it did in the past.

The long-term consequence of a cash-based strategy will invariably be a fall in living standards over time, which means reducing non-essential expenditure such as holidays and entertainment. Inflation rates of 1%, 2% or 7% may not seem much, but it all adds up. During our working life, we are never happy to accept a pay cut. Yet many leave their retirement plans exposed because they limit themselves to cash-based investments. This must be because they do not understand the long-term damage of inflation. In the end, it can be a bitter pill to swallow.

Today, in order to live the lifestyle of a millionaire we need more than a million pounds in the bank. Inflation is

---

9 £1M needed to grow to £3.3M as over the period inflation averaged 4.4%. Source: Office for National Statistics. To have kept up the standard of living, that is the income of £105,000 earned in 1980, the £1,000,000 would have to have grown to £8,764,875 although the income would not have increased over the period.

always with us, and the inflation rate is constantly changing. We cannot accurately predict what lies ahead but we know an inflation rate of 7% means that prices will double every 10 years – a frightening thought if your future income was going to be tied to fluctuating interest rates.

What a difference inflation makes £1Million –the increase in capital needed to keep up		
	5 years	10 years
Inflation at 3%	£1,159,274	£1,343,916
Inflation at 5%	£1,276,282	£1,628,894
Inflation at 7%	£1,402,551	£1,967,151

No-risk inflation-proof investing

Inflation being the enemy of the long-term saver, I am often asked if there is a way of saving to beat inflation without taking any risks. You can. The Government offers index-linked investments that promise to keep up with inflation.

Two types of this kind of investment are currently available – Index-linked gilts, and Index-linked National Savings Certificates. The Savings Certificates are the easiest to understand, as they pay about 1% tax-free on top of the rate of inflation. For example, if inflation is 2%, you get 2% +1%, which is 3%. If inflation is 3%, you get 3% +1%, which is 4%.

If you could invest one million pounds[10] in this risk-free way, the certificates only pay an inflation-adjusted income of

10 There are limits on the amount of NS Certificates you can own

£10,000. Very few of us have saved enough capital to retire on a 1% income.

When choosing investments, the single most important consideration is how they are expected to fare against inflation. The example I used above to compare inflation with a cash deposit from 1980 was selected to emphasise the danger of inflation, rather than a specific criticism of cash. I started an example when interest rates and inflation were high, and I finished it when both were very low.

For a less dramatic view of how cash has performed in comparison to bonds and equities, it is helpful to compare returns over a longer period of time. We can then make a sensible analysis about the best options in a given set of circumstances.

The following table shows how well cash deposits, gilts and equities have performed over the years.

Investment returns relative to inflation (% pa)

Periods measured to the end of 2009

	10 years	20 years	*50 years	*109 years
Equities	-1.5	4.6	5.7	4.9
Gilts	2.4	5.5	2.3	1.2
Index-Linked Gilts	1.9	3.9	n/a	n/a
Cash	2.4	3.5	2. 1	n/a

Gilts had the best ever 20-year return to the end of 2008 beating inflation by 5.5% before tax. Gilts have only rarely outperformed equities over such a long holding period and the situation must have been assisted by the low Bank of England base rate. It dropped to only 0.5%.

The 10-year return for equities was 1.5% below inflation, which was a historical low.

The next table, which uses the full 109 years of stock market data available, shows that investing in equities over ten years was better than cash nine times out of ten. Also, equities were better than gilts eight times out of ten.

Investing for shorter periods reduced the equity advantage. Over a five-year period, equities were better than cash and gilts three-quarters of the time. Reducing the investment time to only three years tipped the scale in favour of gilts.

It would seem the last 10 years were historically unusual as stock markets are 'generally' the best way to invest over 10 years or more. But the word 'generally' includes disasters and the risk of poor years, and so the term should not be used to avoid the obvious point. When investors choose to hold stock market investments for their long term growth potential, they must be prepared for the inevitable poor periods.

The reward for holding equities over a number of consecutive years

	Number of consecutive years				
	2	3	4	5	10
Probability of equities outperforming Cash Deposits	67%	70%	74%	74%	92%
Probability of equities outperforming Gilts	69%	76%	77%	75%	81%

When we make investment decisions, we should make sure the odds are in our favour. When you recognise the danger of inflation, understand the implications of a 7% growth rate, and the likelihood of a long life, you can see that including equities will increase the probability of investing successfully.

The use of historical information has its limits. It does not help us predict what is going to happen next, but it does give a sense of which assets are likely to be better for short term goals, and which are likely to be better over a lifetime.

The evidence indicates that cash should be favoured for short-term investments, whilst equities and gilts should be used in the longer-term.

The stock market's future

THE DRIVING force behind capitalism is business. If capital markets are to keep moving forward, we need a flow of new businesses to replace those that fail. A business will only survive in the long run if it continues to successfully incorporate new technology into the products and services that we buy.

Over time, innovative technologies and the improvement of manufacturing practices has resulted in the mass availability of goods, which were once available only to the wealthy. In short, investment in business is responsible for the rise of living standards in the western world. The economist Joseph Schumpeter noted that silk stockings were once exclusive to the first Queen Elizabeth. It was a capitalist achievement that they eventually became affordable for factory workers, as well as monarchs.

When stock markets have been performing badly, as during the credit crunch, I am often asked, "How do you know stock markets will recover, and be better than cash in the future?"

When you put money into a bank account, the bank then lends your money to someone else. It makes a profit of perhaps 8% more than the interest it pays to you. This is how a traditional bank makes its money – it charges much more to borrowers than it pays to savers.

A bank will only lend money to finance a business if it

believes that the business owners will be able repay the loan in full with interest. On the other side of the transaction a business wishes to borrow because it is confident that it will make enough profit to repay the loan.

Overall, most businesses make enough money to be profitable after paying their bank charges and interest, although some fail.

Would you buy shares in a business if you were not compensated for the risk of it failing, or of it making little profit? If there were no reward for this risk you would put all your money in a bank deposit.

If it is thought a business is high risk in comparison to other investment opportunities, the bank will ask for a higher rate of interest to cover the extra risk. Also, if this company decides to issue more shares to raise capital for expansion, these must be offered at a low price to attract investors, otherwise the investors will buy the shares of less risky companies.

This is the unbreakable link between risk and reward. Investors in equities expect to be rewarded for taking the risk of an uncertain return, and the risk of losing money. When the investment is in a riskier enterprise, the expected reward must be higher.

The fact that companies often fail to make a profit for investors confirms the risk involved. If shares always made more than cash deposits, then there would be no risk.

Stock market returns

Index-linked savings certificates generally pay 1% more than the current rate of inflation. If inflation is 4%, the savings certificate will pay 5%. If inflation then drops to 3%, the certificate will drop to 4%. So the reward, or premium, for the investor is always fixed, risk-free at 1% above inflation.

Academics argue about the reward investors should expect for investing in the stock market compared to the risk-free rate. This reward is called the 'equity risk premium' and it is considered to be about 4% higher than the risk-free rate over the long term. If index linked savings were expected to pay 4%, and they were the standard for a risk-free investment, then the long-term assumption for equities would be 8%.

The historical numbers in the previous section support the principle that stock markets and gilts offer better prospects than cash, as the long-term investor is usually rewarded for taking the risk.

Also, the figures show it is reasonable to expect an 'equity risk premium' of 4% in the long run. Regretfully, this data is often misused by the investment industry.

Managing your own share portfolio

"Investors shouldn't delude themselves about beating the market. They're just not going to do it. It's just not going to happen."
—Daniel Kahneman, Nobel Laureate in Economics, 2002

WHEN YOU come to understand the high costs of portfolio management today, and the absence of market-beating performance from professional fund managers, it is understandable that some will decide to manage their own equity portfolio.

There should only be two risks when you invest in stock markets. The first is the inherent risk of the market itself. It does not matter what shares you own because the whole market can go down. It may fall in anticipation of a recession, or the expectation of high interest rates or a crisis like the dotcom bubble or the credit crunch.

This 'market risk' (or 'systematic risk') is something you cannot avoid, so you must decide the percentage of your savings you are prepared to commit to the stock market. On one hand, this decision will determine the proportion of your savings that will be exposed to stock market downturns. On the other hand, when stock markets perform well, the less you hold in them the less you will make.

The second type of risk is 'company risk' (or 'unsystematic

risk') which is that of choosing companies that perform poorly due to a company specific problem. An example of a company specific problem might be a charismatic chief executive unexpectedly resigning, a shocking profits warning, or the loss of a major customer.

In the academic world, it is universally accepted that diversification is beneficial as it reduces this second risk of investing. It requires us to own a number of different stocks in a portfolio to avoid 'having all your eggs in one basket'.

There is some debate about how many different stocks you will need to minimise the 'company risk' in a portfolio. Some people suggest that a portfolio of 20 stocks provides an investor with sufficient diversification, but this figure is the result of guesswork rather than analysis.

If there are only three shares and one goes bust you wave goodbye to one third of it. If there are only a dozen or so shares and one or two selections perform poorly, these will still have a significant and detrimental effect on a portfolio, during what could be a period of general prosperity for stocks.

Whilst owning only a few shares may result in a massive profit if one of them turns out to be the next Microsoft, the first rule of investing is to avoid the risk of losing money. (The second rule of investing is also to avoid the risk of losing money.)

There is some useful research that confirms a portfolio of 100 stocks is not always sufficient and in recent times the number of shares needed to diversify effectively has increased.[11]

Individual and professional investors both make the same mistakes as they make too many poor individual investment decisions and hold too few stocks, which exposes them to

---

[11] "How Many Stocks Do You Need to be Diversified?" Daniel J. Burnside, Donald R. Chambers, and John S. Zdanowicz, AAII Journal, July 2004.

substantial risks, which on average are not rewarded with higher returns.

Investors would be better selecting shares at random, as does our metaphorical Ape, because most investors are also poor at diversifying. They are biased in favour of certain classes of shares and certain industry sectors. They overlook the unfashionable stocks that often perform well against expectations. As examples, too many investors thought that bank and construction company shares were a bargain just before the credit crunch and that all technology stocks were full of potential just before the dotcom crash.

Another consideration is how practical and cost-effective is it to run a portfolio with such a large number of stocks? A high level of administration is required, there are significant trading costs and investors must keep an accurate record of all the dividends, sales, and purchases for a tax return. Decisions also have to be made with any future rights issues, takeovers and mergers that are likely with any shareholding.

Managing a share portfolio through a stockbroker service is not the ideal solution. There may be an administrative advantage and help consolidating the tax information, but you will be encouraged to trade when it is not in your best interest to do so. You are going to receive a regular supply of recycled and second hand tips written as if you are privy to some special information.

Investors who receive regular monthly information do worse in terms of money earned compared with those who receive only yearly feedback.[12] The receipt of regular information affects their behaviour and encourages them to trade more than they should.

12 Richard H. Thaler, Amos Tversky, Daniel Kahneman, and Alan Schwartz, Quarterly Journal of Economics, May 1997.

Trading is the lifeblood of a stock broking business and the more you trade, the more often a stockbroker can trade in his Bentley Continental for the latest model.

It is not a good idea to manage a share portfolio, other than holding a few shares as a form of entertainment.

> **The misuse of the historical data**
>
> The history we examined in an earlier chapter shows the performance of the stock market indices using the FTSE All share index.
>
> When the media reports stock market gains or losses, the historical figures quoted are usually from the FTSE100 and the FTSE All Share Indices.
>
> The daily news may describe how some companies have had good results or bad results, and if some shares increased in value a lot whilst others collapsed. However, monthly and yearly figures constantly refer to the histories of the FTSE 100 and the FTSE All Share indices.
>
> The reporting of overseas markets always refers to the movements of a major share index such as the S&P 500 in America, the DAX in Germany and the Hang Seng in Hong Kong.
>
> Importantly, these histories are not recording the experiences of those investors who buy and sell individual shares or those with managed funds.
>
> We know that the typical performance of these investors falls short of the index returns, due to poor decision-making and high costs, and yet the prospective customers of stock brokers and active fund managers will often be shown the index returns relative to inflation and deposit account returns. This is wrong if the customer is going to be investing differently.
>
> It is like comparing apples with pears.

SECTION 3
STOCK MARKET STRATEGIES

Picking the best time to invest

"The bank's troubles began when it expanded from its core business and moved into risky investments. When several creditors collapsed, the bank's shares plummeted. One observer said its policies were so reckless, one would think a child would have lent better."

THIS STATEMENT is not from the banking crisis of 2008 but the bankruptcy of a bank called Overend, Gurney & Co. in 1866.[1] Stock market crashes have been with us since the first big crash known as the South Sea Bubble in the 18th century.

Before the 1960s most people thought there must be a way to predict the future price of an investment. If an investor found a way of avoiding a crash, knowing when prices were going to fall and selling up before everyone else, this would be an amazing advantage[2] but if someone did come up with the answer they would be foolish to share this knowledge.

---

1 When the Bank of England declined to support it, the run on the bank turned into a riot. The rot then spread to 10 other banks and 200 companies defaulted on their payments.

2 This is something of a conundrum. A crash occurs when everyone wishes to sell, so prices must fall dramatically to attract buyers. If enough people believed in a system that predicted an imminent crash, and they all sold as a consequence, this would have the effect of bringing forward the date of the crash, so the system would not work

Every stock market crash has its own distinctive features but they all have a similarity. They occur unexpectedly from a period of what appears to be a period of prosperity. With the benefit of hindsight, the feel-good factor was built on shaky foundations. Investor sentiment changes in the blink of an eye and the once-enthusiastic investors begin to sell in panic. What happens is that the perception of a fair price changes and what was once thought a good price to pay for a share is suddenly regarded as too expensive.

The question of what is a fair price for something has been debated for a long time. In the 13th century, St. Thomas Aquinas argued that everything tradable has a fair price, which must be established by common consent. To buy for less than the fair price and then sell for more was inherently wrong. In any normal marketplace, however, there is a balance between buyers and sellers.

Imagine a street with two similar properties for sale and three buyers. The price will rise until one of the buyers drops out. In a falling property market the sellers become more enthusiastic, the number of buyers reduces, and owners must drop the asking price to attract a buyer.

When we think we have bought something for a good price, and regard it as a bargain, this is based on what we believe others will pay for it. This is particularly true for the trader who buys something he doesn't want for himself, but he believes he can sell it to someone else for a future profit. So the behaviour of others matters.

The process of investing with an economic objective is a little like a card player evaluating a poker hand – the value he places in his own cards changes with his estimation of what the other players are holding.

This is why investing can sometimes resemble the game of

'pass the parcel'. For example, an investor buys a City apartment believing others will pay a higher price for it in the near future. People will invest in art, which has no economic value, not only for pleasure but also with the expectation that it will grow in value.

In the right environment, investors will drive up the price of anything that is tradable in the expectation of a short-term profit. Common trading cycles involve art, stamps, wine, gold, classic cars and property,

The stock market can develop a momentum of its own on the way up and the previous 'fair price' of stocks suddenly looks to have been out of place. When one decides to sell, having made a good profit, everything is fine providing there are more than enough buyers who believe that in the future others will buy the same stock at an even higher price.

When observing our actions at this time, it should be noted we are all susceptible to 'confirmation bias', which is the behaviour of hearing what we want to hear and seeing what we want to see. There will be articles in the financial press debating the pros and cons, but the negative ideas are rejected. People may believe they have picked up on some new trend. They can believe the market has not recognised the opportunity. It may be supported by whispers, in pubs and golf clubs, which are interpreted as inside information and the game of pass the parcel gets out of hand.

The beginning of the bull market,[3] which eventually leads to a stock market crash, is often seeded by one of two scenarios.

The first is when we observe rising share prices, which are not supported by any firm economic foundation. The second

---

3 A bull market is associated with increasing investor confidence, and increased investing in anticipation of future price increases

is when there is an expectation of a new technology that will change the world. It may well be that this technology does go on to change the world in the more distant future, but the technology does not meet the investor's short-term profit expectations. It takes much longer to build a profitable business than was originally anticipated and the innovators run out of money before the idea takes off.

It is understandable when a market reacts enthusiastically, particularly when there is a good story to tell, but in these circumstances there has been a triumph of optimism over reality.

Investors anchor the original investment decision around a compelling story that grabs the imagination and no one likes to give up on a good story. It may be about a company that is developing a cure for malaria or cancer, or a new green technology, which becomes the next big trend.

The stories are often so persuasive no one checks out the figures, the real facts are put to one side, and investors acquire a very strong emotional attachment to the stocks they bought on the back of the story. They have come to love the idea but the affection is not rewarded in any way at all.

When discussing the risks investors take by following these trends, they are far too overconfident and all normal standards of reasoning fall by the wayside. Eventually though, there comes a tipping point when reality bursts the bubble of confidence and a crash begins.

Following the dotcom collapse at the start of the century, hindsight tells us that many of the internet investment propositions were pie in the sky. We will never have a perfect knowledge of the future but out of the hundreds of false dotcom promises came Google, Yahoo, Amazon etc. and a change in the way we bank and do business today. The new technologies, for instance, have improved the way I can do my office administration and for less cost.

The only time you can draw a conclusion about market price is when a certain sector of the market increases rapidly due to a fashionable popularity, and common sense says you should avoid the temptation to join the party, because it will end in disaster.

Investors should only commit to investing when they can accept the fact that the first few years could turn out to be very good, average, or very poor and there is no way of knowing which it will be. Over time the general trend of a good investment is upwards and the very good years more than compensate for the poor years.

You will never read, see or hear of a reliable method to tell you when the stock market is priced cheaply or expensively.

Losing money on the back of a good story

'Some people will believe anything they receive in a whisper'

The dot-com bubble provided numerous examples of companies launched on the back of a great story, but if anyone had bothered to look for a viable business model they wouldn't have found one. At the time thousands of investors invested emotionally at great cost to their personal wealth.

Boo.com (1998–2000) – Founded in London as an online fashion store, Boo.com spent $160 million before liquidation.

Flooz.com (1998–2001) – Promoted by Whoopi Goldberg, Flooz was designed as an online currency alternative to credit cards. After buying Flooz credits you could use it as a currency with its retail partners. It raised $35 million before it went bankrupt.

> Pets.com (1998–2000) – This online pet supplies store never gave pet owners a compelling reason to buy its supplies online. Amazon.com backed pets.com and it raised $82.5 million before collapsing.
>
> Kozmo.com (1998–2001) – This online store and delivery service raised $280 million before it closed – laying off 1,100 employees.
>
> Webvan (1999–2001) – This online grocer came to be worth a staggering $1.2 billion at its peak. The grocery business has very small margins and it was never able to attract enough customers. When the company closed it put 2,000 people out of work.

How to miss the best 25 days of your investing life

> *There is an old investment saying that has long served as a guide to trading. "Sell in May and go away, stay away till St Leger's Day."*

This saying promotes the idea that it is a waste of time trading in the summer months. Cynics may say it was a ploy by city traders to have good holidays and enjoy the horse racing season.[4]

Selling in May actually works, often for a number of consecutive years, but just as often it leads to lost opportunities. The summer of 2009 was a very profitable time for stock market investors, which followed a poor winter.

---

4 The St Leger has been run from Doncaster since 1776. There may be some historical basis to the saying because at that time we lived in an agricultural society. September coincided with landowners holding cash from their crops so the winter months were good for banks and traders.

Selling in other months sometimes works too and this gives investors the idea you can identify times when not to be in the stock market, or when to sell gilts or any other type of investment, and then when to reinvest. It is saying you can know the future direction of the price of a share, or oil, or gold, or whatever it is you are studying at the time.

If you try sitting down one wet Sunday, with the idea of reading the financial press, you should notice that a very high percentage of what you see is purely opinion and speculation. You would think that because so many column inches are dedicated to forecasting, that this activity must have some value.

On any day of the week you can pick up a newspaper or investment magazine and there will be experts who write about the stock market being cheap or expensive. When the market has been going down, you will often be encouraged to sell due to the analysis of experts[5] who predict that the market will continue to fall.

Setting the scene, imagine an investor who has been losing money in a falling stock market and he is very unsettled, to the point of feeling ill. He reads the view of a so-called expert[6] in a Sunday paper, who says the market may have even greater falls ahead, and his heart sinks. On Monday, he is very likely to sell everything because the article has stoked

---

5 Occasionally, a journalist will own up. In the Financial Times 'Traders Diary' column, the stock market historian David Schwartz wrote, "Spotting bear market bottoms in real-time is a dangerous game. My recent efforts at bottom picking went painfully wrong. I am now a bit gun shy about calling another bear bottom"

6 There is always someone willing to tell us how to identify the next winner. When such views are published it is worth asking, "If it is such a good idea why would the writer share it with others?" If there really is some secret information the sooner it gets out the sooner it fails to be a secret and everybody will soon catch up.

HOW TO INVEST BETTER THAN THE AVERAGE PRIMATE

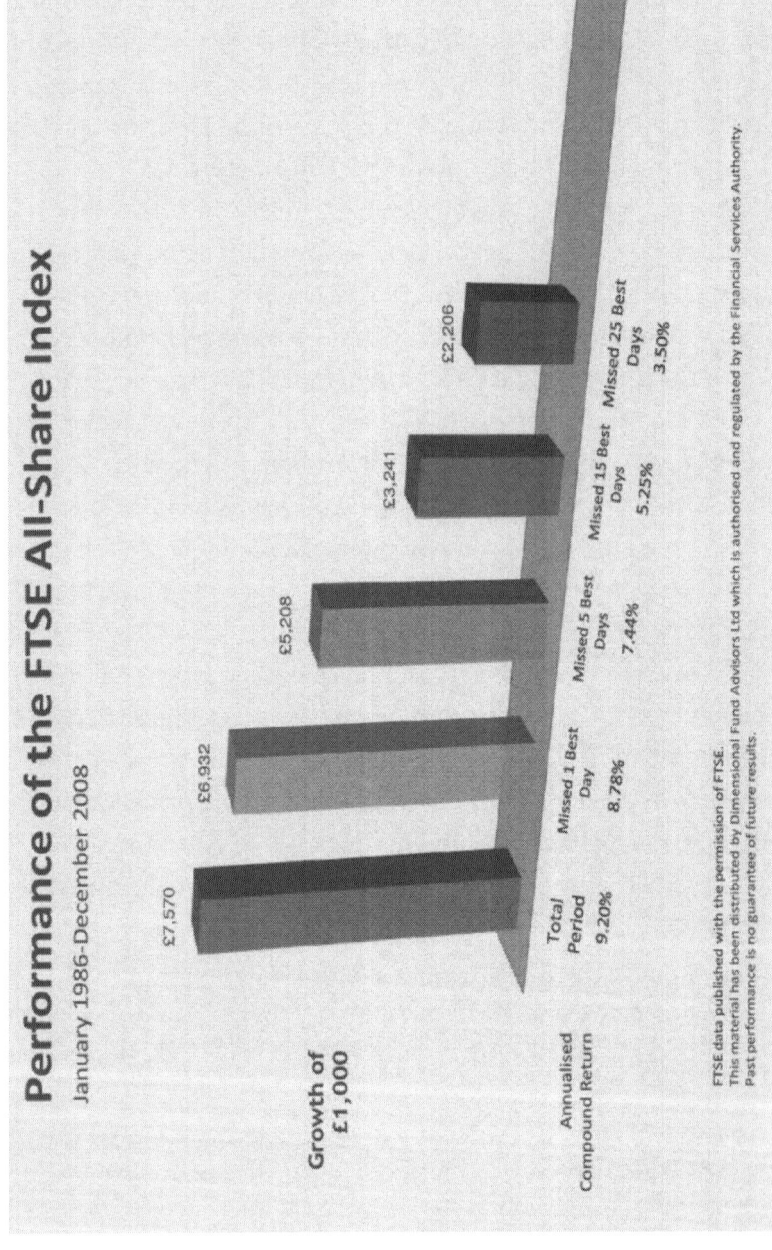

up his aversion to losses. The consolation, he tells himself, is the chance of recouping his losses when he buys the investments back just as the market is about to recover. Could it be a reasonable idea to sell, having already suffered a loss, with an idea of buying the investments back later?

Have a look at the adjacent table and see how investing in the UK stock market looked over a 23 year time frame. You can see, with hindsight how quickly the profit declined by missing a few good days.

But how could you possibly identify the best 25 days out of 23 years, or put another way, the best single day in the year?

If you had missed only the best five days during 23 years, the investment return is 1.8% less every year for the entire 20-year period. It would also be wonderful to miss the worst day in every year, but identifying this day cannot be any easier.

If you considered an idea that you can make a profit by coming out of the market when you think it is going down, and returning when you think it is going up again then you will need to do this successfully for many consecutive years to beat the market return.

In reality, you are more likely to win the national lottery than succeed in predicting the top and bottom of the market in real time. The fact is that most people sell their investments *after* suffering a loss during a crash, not because they successfully anticipated the fall.

Do not leave at half time

I was once invited to a football match. I am not a football fan, but I like watching sport. My host said, "Come along! It's a great day out and you'll enjoy yourself. The team lets in a few goals, but our attack is lethal and in the end we'll score even more." We took our seats in a good spot, so that we were only a short flight of stairs away from the snack bar. The first 20 minutes were uneventful and the anticipated goals did not materialise, not even a shot on goal or a poor decision by the referee to lift the tedium. My host, obviously getting agitated, assured me it was going to get better. Another 20 minutes of tedium followed.

I was thankful for the suggestion to forget the last five minutes of the first half to get a coffee before the rush. We went to the bar, ordered our drinks, and then the crowd roared. Such was the excitement, the whole stand seemed to be rocking and without hesitation my friend had hurled himself up the stairs to try and see the goal he had just missed! Apparently, it was the goal of the season and the match ended 1-0.

The point of this story is that my friend, whose knowledge of football is vast, decided it was not worth watching the last five minutes of the first half. His good memories of all the exciting matches he had watched were erased during the first 40 minutes and he misjudged the future of the game. His decision cost him the sight of the best goal of the season.[7]

It is not just that football fans soon get fed up when things aren't going well as investors react in exactly the same way. Stock markets are often poor for lengthy periods, and investors very quickly lose patience after a downturn. Heavy selling drives market downturns and then a recovery arrives unexpectedly and quickly. They miss the best of the action.

---

[7] The most famous turnaround in recent times was in a European Cup final game in Istanbul 25th May 2005. Liverpool was 3-0 down at half time. At this point most of the Liverpool fans walked out of the ground, only to miss the second half reply of 3 goals in six minutes. Milan lost the match during the penalty shootout.

PICKING THE BEST TIME TO INVEST

Many of those who sell after making a loss stay on the fence during a recovery phase, because they believe they could be observing what might be a short-term upswing. They will read commentaries in newspapers to support their doubts as the market continues upwards.

Eventually they capitulate and reinvest in fear of missing out. They return only because of commentaries about the market *'doing'* well but they are using the wrong tense. These latecomers should be noting, 'The market has *done* well'. They have invested after the first goal has been scored, and it may be months before there are any more good investing days.

If you miss only a handful of the 'few good days', then you will have missed out. The way to be profitable is to 'stay in your seat'. Do not try to time the market.

How do professional investors work?

"It is better for a reputation to fail conventionally than to succeed unconventionally."

—John Maynard Keynes

PROFESSIONALS ARE obsessed with benchmarking, which is a method of comparing their performance against the other fund managers in the market. The great majority are sophisticated investors but they are all subject to the same biases.

You would expect most professionals to try to outperform the market. However, research indicates that in the mainstream fund management industry, outside of the hedge fund and other specialist areas, the majority are interested in minimising the risk to their careers, and so they do not try to outperform the rest. In effect they follow each other's behaviour and they behave like a herd.

Professionals generally use the same methods of analysis; they will employ similar mathematical models and theories. The great weakness is that these tools will work only most of the time. They are incomplete, because they do not anticipate future stock market crashes, and the often-long periods during which it is difficult to show a profit. They persist in trying to beat each other, even though the facts show their methods rarely lead to market-beating success stories.

In truth, many professionals are hampered by their elegant and hard to understand models, and like individual investors, the professionals become overconfident about their abilities.

There are only two ways a very active professional can make more than the others. The first is to have inside information, which is illegal, and the second is to have superior forecasting skills. Either way it involves making bold decisions. Those who try are so often wrong about the future, they regularly underperform the market. They also change their minds a lot judging by the amount of high-volume, high-cost trading that takes place.[8]

Investors who buy specialist actively managed funds are often unfortunate, because they are exposed to 'company risk' due to the poor level of diversification. Such fund managers actively pick companies they expect to outperform, and avoid the companies they do not like, and therefore they avoid investing in the many stocks that would otherwise have provided the diversity to spread the risk.

They also attempt to make judgements about stock markets being at a fair price, cheap, or expensive and as a result they often miss a good market run.[9] So investors suffer a third level of risk, which we could label as 'management error'.

I have seen estimates that specify between 80% and 90%

---

8 During 2008 the average portfolio turnover for UK Core equity funds was 63%. Source: Fitzrovia Portfolio Turnover of UK Funds December 2008.

9 During the stock market recoveries that started in March 2003 and March 2009, following the dot-com crash and the credit crunch respectively, a large percentage of actively managed funds underperformed during the recovery due to management error. The reason was widely reported to be due to managers holding a high percentage of cash and what were considered to be defensive stocks.

of all professional investment activity revolves around forecasting and we know there is no evidence this works much at all. Curiously, although most professionals manage funds on the basis that the markets are efficient, a very high percentage of them believe the markets are irrational[10] which somewhat contradicts the assumptions of their own models.

The pursuit of outperformance leads both individuals and professionals to make judgements about whether the stock market is expensive and if individual stock prices represent good value. They will decide how the present price of stocks relates to their judgement of the 'correct' prices. They will reduce their stock holdings when they are considered to be expensive and they will plan to buy them back after prices have gone down and they appear to be cheap again.

The ultimate goal of market timing is to avoid the next crash. The point that no UK fund management groups I know have succeeded in avoiding them in the past confirms the idea is dead in the water.

---

10 A CFA survey indicated 67% do not believe the market is rational.

Charts and the search for patterns

"When our ancestors first roamed the countryside our sight and our senses were developed to spot small movements on a distant horizon. We learned to recognise the seasonal patterns in order to survive."

IF YOU try tossing a coin to get a series of 10 heads or tails in a row it may take about a thousand attempts. If you get a group of people, and they have the enthusiasm to keep at it, you will get one or two who get heads or tails 15 or 20 times a row.

On the other hand, if we are asked to imagine tossing a coin and then to write down a fictitious set of results, we will not usually write down ten heads or tails in a row although this is a series that will happen just as often as any other combination we might commit to paper.

Our imaginary series would never include such a long string of heads or tails because when we do see such a pattern we look to give it a cause, which plainly does not exist if it is a simple matter such as heads or tails.

This leads us to the pseudoscience known as Technical Analysis, which is the study of patterns in charts. It is said to be a discipline to assist the forecasting of the future direction of prices through the study of past market data, usually the price of trades and a volume of trades.

The analysts using charts say the patterns can be studied, and knowledge of previous patterns is a guide to the future direction of the stock market, the price of gold, house prices etc. These types of charts are published and discussed at length and there are many users.

Academics have said the evidence for technical analysis is vast and inconsistent.[11] A review of studies on technical analysis reported a number of positive results but that many of these positive results were doubtful.[12]

The following is an example of a chart showing how you might analyse the historic movement of a company share to determine its future price direction. It shows three identifiable observations used by chartists during the process of technical analysis. The first is a double top, and then a resistance level followed by an uptrend.

11 Quote: Eugene Fama, Professor of Finance at the University of Chicago Booth School of Business
12 Irwin, Scott H. and Park (2007). What Do We Know About the Profitability of Technical Analysis? *Journal of Economic Surveys*, Vol. 21, No. 4, pp. 786-826.

Professor Burton Malkiel tells a story of how he fooled a friend, who was a technical analyst, by showing him a chart that was generated by coin tosses. He led him to believe he was looking at actual stock prices and the friend wanted to know the name of the stock.[13] I have just repeated the exercise, as the above chart is just another example of coin tossing results.[14]

It has been observed that people who feel out of control are more likely to see illusionary patterns in stock market data.[15] I think it is a simple matter of chartists studying random patterns, and trying to make something out of nothing, which is a weakness to be found in all of us.

There is a phenomenon known as Momentum, which a chartist would wish to identify. It is based on an observation that when the price of a stock has just gone up (or the price of gold, or property etc. has gone up), it often seems to keep going up. Conversely when it is going down it seems to keep going down. The idea has some support from academic analysis, but unfortunately it is unlikely you could ever profit from it.

'Jumping on the bandwagon', is not often profitable, as was confirmed by a test done by Investors Chronicle. It backtested a momentum strategy over a five-year period. Although the system had some success, and it outperformed the UK stock market, the high cost of the numerous transactions wiped out all of the gains.

13 Malkiel is a professor of economics at Princeton University and author of 'A Random Walk down Wall Street'
14 Source: A blog of Excel tips and tricks by Timothy R. Mayes, Ph.D. a faculty member in the Finance Department at Metropolitan State College of Denver.
15 Jennifer Whitson of the University of Texas at Austin and Adam Galinsky of Northwestern University in Evanston, Illinois. Source: Science, vol. 322, p 115

SECTION 4
BUILD YOUR OWN PORTFOLIO

Achieving success is easier than a round of golf

YOU DESERVE the market return on your savings. This means that when you hold money in a cash deposit account you are entitled to earn a good rate of interest. If you invest into bonds you deserve a competitive rate of interest without the risk of losing your capital and if you invest in stock markets you must make sure you profit in line with the market.

Far too many people pay for the privilege of investment advice and take the risks of investing but they do not get the market return. However, achieving a successful investment experience is much easier than trying to achieve success in any sport I know. I will use the great game of golf as a good example.

Imagine if someone could show you how to play every championship golf course in the world and hit par. You are going to play at any golf course and never lose your ball. Every par three, no matter how difficult, is always going to take three shots. Every club player I have met, will play three, four or five holes well and then hit a frustrating shot out of bounds, or hook a shot into the pond at the back of the green. On a windy day, or when it's raining or snowing, you would never suffer these annoyances.

If you study every average golfer they make plenty of good

shots in a round of golf, but far too many mistakes. When they 'lose it' after making a couple of bad shots, they will often try too hard and be over ambitious in an effort to make up for the last mistake. Instead of settling for one over par after a bad shot, they end up two or even three over par on one hole. Two or three bad holes lead to a bad round and no prizes.

The investment equivalent of the golf skill I have just described is indexing, which is accepting the market return. It eliminates the costly mistakes active investors make when trying to out-perform the market index. It avoids making the equivalent of a shot into the pond or out of bounds. Unlike the ability to play golf to such a high standard, and perhaps surprisingly, it is not as difficult to achieve the same level of investing excellence.

If it is reasonable to expect the return on bonds to be 4% in the long run and the return on equities to be 8% there will always be a majority of investors looking for more, for example, 6% from bonds and 12% from the stock market. They use trading systems, market timing, stock selection, hunches and technical analysis etc. in the quest for outperformance. Unfortunately, these ideas do not work for long. They come unstuck and they lose money.

These are all similar to taking a wild swing at golf. Sometimes it works, but the trouble is that you must be very consistent to succeed over the full round. It only takes one big investing error, or a plausible idea that was flawed in its execution and you are behind the index return. One mistake leads to another and before long you are staring at a miserable round of investing.

I have described the many different ways in which investors attempt to beat the market index. The reality is that attempts to beat the market will consistently end in failure.

On the other hand, when an investor links their investments to an index such as the FTSE100 or the FTSE All Share index they are buying into what the market considers the best businesses ranked by size. The reason these companies are in the index is because they are the ones supported by investors and judged by the consensus view to be the best and most valuable companies.

> ### Stock markets are constantly changing
>
> The FTSE 100 index is the most widely quoted UK stock market indicator. It is maintained by the FTSE group. The top 100 companies represent about 80% of the UK stock exchange, and they are weighted according to their size. This means a larger company will make more of a difference to the index compared to smaller company when its share price moves up or down. The smallest company in the FTSE 100 will be worth approximately £1.7 billion at the time of writing.
>
> The FTSE All-Share is also a weighted index. It represents the performance of the London Stock Exchange's main market and at the time of writing it included 619 companies and 98% of the stock market's value. The FTSE All-Share Index is considered to be the best performance measure of the London stock market.
>
> The indices are constantly changing. For example the FTSE 100 index changes four times a year. The changes represent the fortunes of companies growing and shrinking in a changing marketplace. Companies are taken over, or they merge, or they go bust. Others come to prominence and grow because they have identified and satisfied the demand for new products and services, or new ways of delivering what we want.

An index fund always follows the supply and demand of the market. The top 100 companies that make up the FTSE 100 index are selected as a result of the collective actions of all the traders in the city, overseas investment institutions, and individual investors worldwide. Institutions spend tens of millions of pounds every year in research, so beating all these resources is going to be extremely difficult, and it is only going to happen through luck.

The FTSE 100 index is totally different to how it looked when it started in 1984. For example, Woolworths joined in 1984, as did the furniture company MFI and Eagle Star insurance, none of which is trading today. An index fund is not at all static as it constantly adjusts to reflect market changes, and it keeps moving with the times.

The same applies with all of the world's main indices and the rate of change has been increasing in recent years.[1]

When you understand this rate of change you can cast aside the first criticism of index funds, usually made by the casual observer that following an index cannot be very smart. Surely a few very clever traders working together can beat the market? Well they can, but as the previous chapters have shown, not that often.

Some investors cannot see the sense of owning a tracker fund that will follow a market when it goes down. Again, the evidence shows that compared to the experience of most investors, this is an acceptable outcome. The majority of investors

---

1 The changes in the FTSE100 are listed in the appendix. They have increased by 25% since the first five years 1984/88 and the five-year period ending 2004/8. In America the top 500 companies, as measured by the 'Fortune 500', have been much more mobile. Between 1956-81 an average of 24 firms dropped out of the list every year and by 1982-2006 that number had jumped to 40.

do a lot worse than the market during a downturn because their funds underperform or they buy and sell at the wrong time.

The foundation for your portfolio should be index investing.

How to beat the professional investor

"The most powerful force in the universe is compound interest"
—Albert Einstein

THERE IS a problem for investors of modest means wishing to build a decent investment portfolio. Speaking to a financial planner with expertise in this area is unlikely to be productive because the fees will outweigh the benefits.

It seems the only option is to deal with investment sales people, who are motivated by commission, but you cannot accept such advice with confidence as the products offered are often expensive and of doubtful quality. Instead, you should build your own simple portfolio.

The D-I-Y portfolios described below are suitable for those with capital up to £60,000. Buying your own investments will continue to work for larger portfolios but a limiting factor will be the availability of National Savings Certificates and the need to buy other defensive assets.

The D-I-Y portfolios will put you at a great advantage over the great majority of investors who do not know their investing costs or understand their exposure to risk. Your investments will minimise the starting up, or initial costs and trading costs, and the risks are controlled with a mix of stock market and government investment bonds.

You will also have a realistic measure of the longer term return you can expect and it is good to be patient as get rich quick schemes do not work. The longer you leave the portfolio to grow the longer you will have for the returns to build up due to the effect of compounding, in the same way that compound interest builds up over time.

We start our plans with the understanding that we have no control over stock markets or interest rates, that there is no way of forecasting accurately and that market timing does not work. Also, we know we have no way to control the behaviours and opinions of others.

However, we can manage our own investing behaviour, asset allocation and exposure to risk.

> **The characteristics of your Portfolio**
>
> Low costs
>
> Less volatility
>
> Discipline, to protect you from making big mistakes
>
> A deep understanding of investing is not required
>
> Earn the market returns you deserve

Plan your short term savings first

"A bird in the hand is worth two in the bush"

YOUR PORTFOLIO must suit your own circumstances and match investment risks with your goals. Before making any longer term investment decisions you should start with your short-term plans and write them down.

This does not have to be complex, as the main aim is to quantify the cash requirement for your short-term goals. Only then should you progress to plan for your longer-term goals.

Cash is the only way to invest for short-term spending needs. Short-term is definitely three years, and depending on your perception of risk and how important the goal is to be fulfilled, short term may mean five years. For example, if you are funding a child's higher education, and there are no other savings to call on, cash deposits are the solution. However, the education fund could use a fixed rate deposit of one year, two years[2] etc. to earn an extra rate of interest.

By holding cash for the short term you miss the opportunity to earn good stock market returns. You also avoid the risk of not being able to fund your short-term liabilities in the event of a stock market fall.

2 Plan carefully to avoid the danger of having money tied up when you might need it.

Your Portfolio

THE FOUNDATION is a fund tracking the FTSE All Share Index combined with Index-Linked National Savings Certificates. This portfolio provides a good solution, with little risk of making an error. If you have the ability to use online banking, or sort out your insurance online then you have the ability to build this portfolio and it's variations to fit your circumstances.

Later on I describe a second version. If you have no investment experience at all, I suggest sticking with the simpler portfolio until the second year of investing. By then you will have gained some knowledge and confidence.

Index linked National Savings Certificates (IL CERTS) are bonds guaranteed by the Government so they are risk free. The investor can choose IL CERTS with either a three-year or five-year investment period, or a mix of both.

The terms of each new issue of certificates will vary, but the returns for each issue are fixed for the duration of the contract. It is important to invest for the full period to receive the full inflation return plus the bonus. At maturity, the certificates can be rolled over into another certificate.

The assumption is that IL CERTS will return your capital, plus tax-free interest equal to the rate of inflation, plus 1%. For example, if inflation averaged 3%, an investor will earn 4%. There have been times when the return has been less than inflation plus 1%, and times when it has been much higher, but the 1% reward is a sensible working assumption for the future.

The table below shows the returns of the FTSE index fund for the 20 years ending December 2009. These 20 years will not be repeated but they can be used to demonstrate the risks and rewards that come with stock market investing, as this was a period of two quite different halves.

In the charts that follow it is assumed the investor achieves a return of the All Share index less a fund charge of 1% per annum.[3]

A stock market fund 20 years to 2009

Year	FTSE All Share fund
1990	**-10.6**
1991	19.5
1992	19.2
1993	27.1
1994	**-6.8**
1995	22.5
1996	15.5
1997	22.3
1998	12.6
1999	22.9
2000	**-6.8**
2001	**-14.1**
2002	**-23.4**
2003	19.6
2004	11.7
2005	20.8
2006	15.5
2007	4.2
2008	**-30.6**
2009	23.9

---

[3] There is a good selection of All Share index funds with an annual cost of 1% or below. This is discussed in the appendix.

The first 10 years of investing were exceptionally profitable, although the decade started with an unsettling first-year loss of over 10%. There were only two years of losses, and as these fell between very profitable years, investors would not have been too concerned. The stock market investor had a great time as the fund comfortably trebled value.

The second period was a total contrast. It started with three years of losses, and good years were thin on the ground. The penultimate year, 2008, had an unsettling loss of over 30%. After 10 years of investing the stock market investor would have just about broken even at the finish thanks to an excellent 2009.

The Growth of £1,000 – 20 years to 2009

Year	Growth of £1,000	Year	Growth of £1,000
1990	892	2000	931
1991	1,068	2001	798
1992	1,276	2002	609
1993	1,626	2003	730
1994	1,515	2004	816
1995	1,860	2005	988
1996	2,151	2006	1,144
1997	2,636	2007	1,193
1998	2,973	2008	824
1999	£3,663	2009	£1,022

Although the history of stock market investing shows this second ten-year period is not typical, it serves as a reminder of what can happen, and before investing you should understand the risks of your chosen strategy as well as the potential rewards.[4]

As there is no way of knowing in advance if your investment portfolio is starting just before a good period or a poor one, the portfolio must have a way of limiting the downside risk so you can tolerate the poor years when they arrive.

For the majority of investors, a portfolio invested entirely in the stock market is uncomfortably volatile. It is easy to imagine earning the 1995 return of 22.5% or the 2009 return of 23.9% but how would you feel and how would you react if your first three-year experience was a loss of over 40%, which many investors experienced between 2000 and 2003 before they ran for cover?

It is because so many investors did not have any idea of the investment risks they were taking that they became terrified and sold their investments. The biggest mistake is to start investing without understanding what you are doing, and then to abandon, or significantly change the strategy. Often, investors run away just in time to miss an unexpected recovery.

Adding the IL CERTS is beneficial for the times when stock markets are poor because you reduce your losses. The following table shows that such a portfolio with a 50 – 50 split would have lost less than15% in 2008, which was by far the worst of the last 20 years. During periods of high inflation and poor stock market returns the cushioning effect works very well. In 1990 the portfolio would have shown a very small loss during a year when equities were down over 10%.

---

[4] It would be quite easy to study other periods in time, and every one of them is different. It becomes a dangerous pastime when we try to base our future investment strategy on a chain of events that occurred previously, and applying the ideas that would have worked then, with the benefit of hindsight.

The 50/50 portfolio return

Year	FTSE All Share fund	IL CERTS	50% of each
1990	**-10.6**	10.4	**-0.1**
1991	19.5	5.5	12.5
1992	19.2	3.6	11.4
1993	27.1	2.9	15.0
1994	**-6.8**	3.9	**-1.5**
1995	22.5	4.2	13.4
1996	15.5	3.5	9.5
1997	22.3	4.6	13.5
1998	12.6	3.7	8.2
1999	22.9	2.7	12.8
2000	**-6.8**	3.9	**-1.5**
2001	**-14.1**	1.7	**-6.2**
2002	**-23.4**	3.9	**-9.8**
2003	19.6	3.8	11.7
2004	11.7	4.5	8.1
2005	20.8	3.2	12.0
2006	15.5	5.4	10.5
2007	4.2	5.0	4.6
2008	**-30.6**	1.9	**-14.4**
2009	23.9	1.3	12.6

Chart of the 20-year period ending 2009

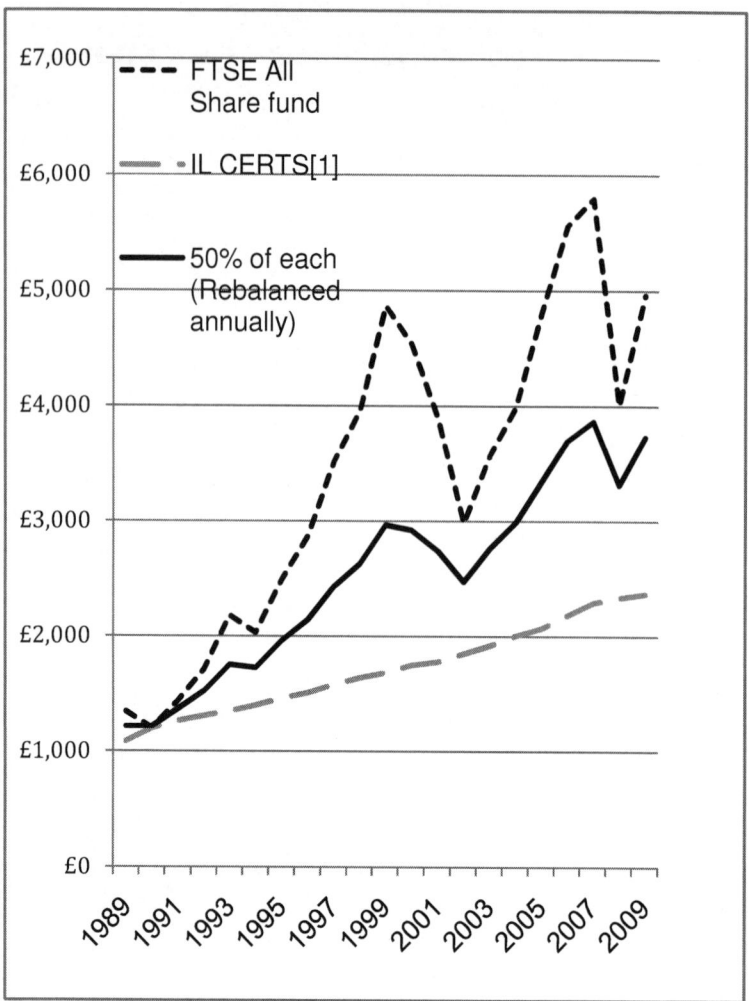

[1] RPI +1%

Over 20 years the balanced 50/50 portfolio offered a return that was comfortably above inflation, and it was much less volatile than the stock market portfolio. In the real world of investing a 50-50 portfolio is much easier to live with when the times are bad.

Think of your investment decision as being similar to choosing the type of car you wish to use on an unfamiliar journey. You could buy a sports model that has the capability to get you to your destination quickly providing the roads are good, or a 4x4, which will reach your destination over rougher terrain.

Your investment vehicle is likely to be better if you select a mix of investments. The stock market investment provides the growth when the investment journey is good, and the defensive IL CERTS give reassurance when the journey is difficult.

A 50-50 portfolio is a good starting point from which you can change the mix to suit your own investment requirements.

If you are cautious, and your investment strategy does not demand a high investment return, you could select 25% stock market and 75% IL CERTS. If you are not too concerned about short-term volatility and need a higher return you can select 75% stock market and 25% IL CERTS. Remember that the choices are almost endless and you could choose any mix.

Table: 20 years to Dec 2009 – the best and worst years[5]

FTSE All share fund %	IL CERTS %	Best year %	Worst year %
75%	25%	28.1	-22.9
50%	50%	21.4	-15.0
25%	75%	15.0	-6.7

5 All figures are rounded down to one decimal place. The figures are for portfolios that are rebalanced annually (rebalancing is explained in the next section)

The $50,000 question – how did we do?

"A child who buys ILNS certificates from the Post Office is likely to have a more profitable investment experience than the typical stock market investor."

OVER THE 20-year period to December 2009, my 50/50 portfolio would have produced an annualised average return of 6.5%, and beaten inflation by 3.3% a year. This is net of costs. Had an investor decided to accept the high volatility of the FTSE All Share index fund, the annualised average return would have increased to 7.8%, which is 4.6% above inflation.

This compares exceptionally well with the experience of the typical investor who suffered a 'performance gap' of over 2%, because they end up with poor performing and expensive funds.

Unfortunately, this is only one half of the story, because investors are encouraged to trade, and to buy and sell inappropriately, and this behaviour is estimated to lose them another 2% a year, so the total performance gap is over 4% a year. So they did not get even close to matching the 7.8% earnings of the index fund.

The FTSE index fund earned 7.8%, when the typical investor earned only about 3.8%, a lower return than IL CERTS, which returned 4.2% over the 20 year period.

THE $50,000 DOLLAR QUESTION – HOW DID WE DO?

The strategies compared – 1990-2009

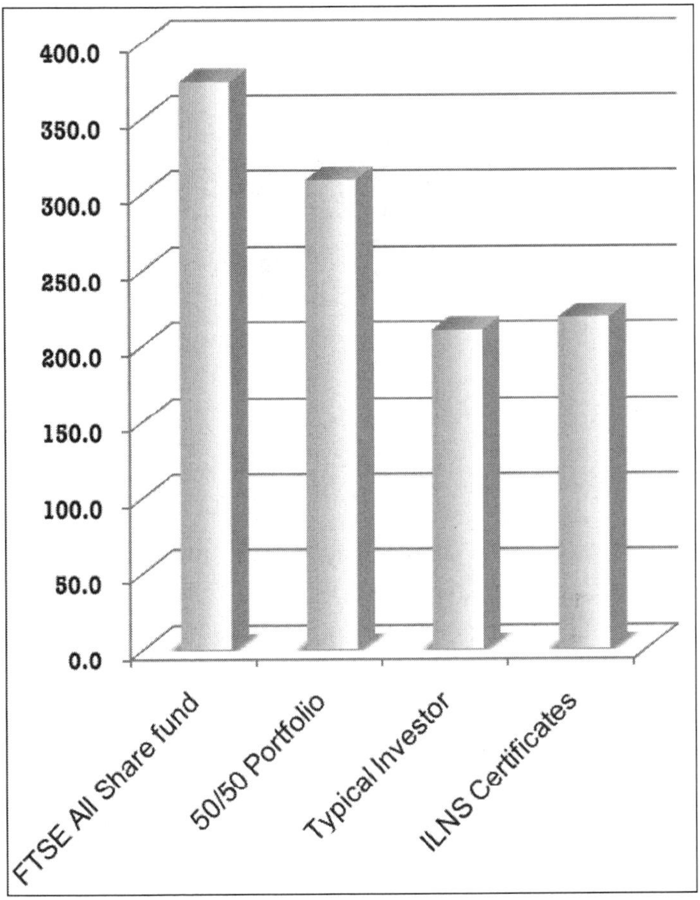

(Bar chart showing values for: FTSE All Share fund ~380, 50/50 Portfolio ~310, Typical Investor ~210, ILNS Certificates ~220)

The figures I use in the chart above are based on the long-term research competed by the legendary Vanguard founder John Bogle whose research covered the American stock market and a study of the UK market between 1992 and 2003 by Lukas Schneider of DFA's London office.[6] I have seen

---

[6] The author has taken the liberty of extrapolating the only available UK data from 1992-2003 over the full 20-year period. The long term data from America which runs from 1984 suggests this is a perfectly reasonable approach to make.

all this research mentioned on numerous occasions and I have never seen any comment that tries to make out the conclusions are incorrect.

By constructing your own DIY portfolio you can rest assured that your results could comfortably beat the majority of investors without all of that wasted effort. Those who follow star fund managers, and move from one investing trend to another, earn much less than the market return and they pay out more.

Importantly, you earn the returns that many would envy and your hard earned money is not exposed a higher level of risk.

Adding diversity

The DIY portfolio can be taken to a second level. IL CERTS continue as the defensive asset class, but my variation recognises the fact that the UK stock market accounts for less than 10% of global stock markets.

There are many UK companies trading around the world, but restricting the investment strategy to the UK denies you the opportunity of sharing in the profits of the world's greatest businesses.

The more companies you have in your portfolio the greater the diversity, which means more metaphorical eggs in many different baskets.

To achieve this additional diversity, you can substitute the trusted FTSE All Share fund with an international index fund that includes the UK as a part of its geographical spread, or you combine the FTSE All Share fund with an international fund excluding the UK.

The advantage of having the two equity funds is that of being able to control how much of your portfolio you wish to have invested in the UK and how much you wish to be invested in overseas markets. Most investors I meet exhibit 'home bias', preferring to have a much higher percentage than 10% in the UK.

The disadvantage of adding the international fund is that it requires more research and care in its construction. The reward for the effort is that you can expect less volatility. The only times a UK portfolio would consistently beat a global portfolio will be if the UK stock market was the best performing stock market or Sterling was the strongest currency for a number of years on the trot.

Looking forward to the expected investment returns

Risk and reward go hand-in-hand. If you select a strategy entirely of IL CERTS you know you will have a certain investment return of 1% above inflation, and you should not be disappointed or surprised with the result. This could be a return as low as 1%, if inflation was zero, or 4% if inflation was 3%.

When you buy a stock market fund you expect to be rewarded for the risk, which is that of having an uncertain return each year. An acceptable assumption, to use in your planning, is for stock market funds to earn 4% more than the IL CERTS[7] over the long run.

---

7 4% is a widely used assumption and it is known as the 'equity risk premium'. However, it would be more usual to refer to the equity risk premium as being 4% above the return of T-Bills, which have a higher long term expected return then the ILNS Certificates. In this context the assumptions are conservative.

A T-Bill (Treasury Bill) is a debt instrument issued by the Government with a duration of one year or less. They do not pay interest as they are issued at a discount. T-Bills are generally used as the benchmark for calculating 'the risk free rate'.

If our assumption for inflation is 3%, with IL CERTS earning 4%, the stock market returns will offer 4% more, a figure of 8%. However, we should deduct the 1% annual management fee, and therefore assumption for stock market funds is a return of 7%.

The most important factor for the longer-term investor is the assumed rate of return above inflation. With inflation at 7%, the assumed growth of a 50-50 portfolio is 9.5%, whereas the figure is only 5.5% when assuming 3% inflation. In reality, both figures are the same after deducting the rate of inflation.

Expected returns with inflation at 3%

FTSE All share fund %	Return assumption %	Return less inflation
100%	7.0	4.0
75%	6.2	3.2
50%	5.5	2.5
25%	4.7	1.7
100% IL CERTS	4.0	1.0

Expected returns with inflation at 7%

FTSE All share fund %	Return assumption %	Return less inflation
100%	11.0	4.0
75%	10.2	3.2
50%	9.5	2.5
25%	8.7	1.7
100% IL CERTS	8.0	1.0

Although these figures are modest, I believe they reflect the long-term reality of investing. After studying reams of historical data, I would say that a portfolio with 50% to 60% stock market content would do well to beat inflation by 3% in the long run. In this context, holding only cash over the longer term is often disastrous.[8]

When using assumptions it is good to keep in the front of your mind that we are not dealing with an accurate forecast. You may remember Mister Spock from Star Trek saying something like, "It's approximately 14.732634 microns Jim." Spock was actually giving a very accurate figure from a human perspective, but our assumptions will never actually be correct, as stock market returns and inflation are so variable.

If you see return assumptions written to two decimal places, do not be misled by such spurious accuracy. The purpose of using an assumption is to guide us when we ask questions such as 'will my money run out?' or 'how much do I need to save for my financial independence?' without being overly optimistic or pessimistic.

Do not get bogged down in calculations – the important point is to get started with your planning. You can fine-tune it when you review it.

---

[8] The figures also emphasise the importance of buying funds with low costs. Investors who buy stock market funds and bond funds with high costs will struggle to out-perform inflation over the longer term, as the previous section demonstrated. Fund managers who run up costs of 2% or more a year are taking far too much away from the investor. The author reconfirms the point that investors would be better off with ILNS Certificates rather than expensive and volatile equity funds.

The 4-stage action Plan

> Plan > Implement > File > Review

Write down a plan to identify your goals and priorities, set aside cash for short-term needs and emergencies, and choose the split between the FTSE All Share Fund and IL CERTS.

The asset allocation you choose may end up being a compromise, for instance, having to take more risk than you would wish for in a perfect world, to give you a reasonable expectation of meeting your goals.

> Purchase an FTSE All Share Fund (or an international index fund). There is help with fund selection in the appendix. Purchase a three or five year IL CERTS on line or at a Post Office.

After completing the investments keep all your records together either password protected on your computer (and backed up) or in a single paper file (which if stolen gives no access to your account passwords.

> Diary forward one year and resist the temptation to make changes during the year based on what you hear and read in the news. After one year review your plan, review your allocation, and continue investing after rebalancing the investment

Leave them to grow

When I was a student, I worked in a fancy goods shop in Blackpool during one of the summer holidays. Every morning we were run off our feet as people walked down to the beach and to the famous 'Golden Mile'. We experienced a similar rush when they returned to their hotels when the sun retreated.

During the day we were quiet after the hour or so needed to restock and we used the time to recharge our batteries. However, when the area manager's car pulled up outside, we always looked busy. One of us would sweep the floor; another would go up a stepladder to tidy the shelves, whilst another made noises in the back yard to simulate moving boxes and rubbish.

The shelves were already tidy, the floor was already clean, and the waste was tidy so all our activity served no real purpose except to impress the boss. We all did our jobs well and the only person who thought it was necessary to charge around all day was the area manager.

In a similar way, too many investors will be busy checking their portfolios every weekend, and feel they must do some trading every week and keep busy.

Your life is much easier. You leave your savings well alone, allowing them to do their job in between the annual reviews.

Case studies – the first year

Case study 1

The short-term investor

John has saved a few thousand pounds to pay for next year's family holiday. By booking early he fixed a low price and only has to pay a small deposit now and the balance four weeks before he travels.

This means he can invest £3,000 until he has to make the final payment. Assuming £20 notes under the mattress is not a serious option, where should he invest his holiday money?

He reads the newspapers and the overwhelming 'consensus opinion' is that the stock market is looking good for the next 12 months and there are many opportunities to make big money. He also sees that a bank deposit pays only 1%.

In this context, investing in stocks is a bad idea. History tells us that investing in the stock market for three years or less has only a two in three chance of beating cash, or put another way a one in three chance of losing money, sometimes a lot of money. He cannot afford to lose money because then there will be a shortfall and no holiday, unless he is prepared to borrow the difference.

In this example, a cash deposit guarantees he will meet his goal of going on holiday but he accepts the amount of interest will be small, perhaps only enough to pay for the airport coffee.

Any other investing idea, even though there is a chance of a profit to cover all his holiday spending money, is a really bad bet to make.

Case study 2

The careful young parent

Ruth has no investment experience but managed to put together a written financial plan. It was worked out over the course of two weekends, so she could think it through carefully, and the written process has helped her to line up her financial goals in life.

Her son and daughter are both under five years of age. Her main goal is to help them through university and to give each of them a good start in life by providing a deposit for their first house.

Provision has already been made for some essential home improvements within the next 12 months and for a change of car within the next three years. Margaret has short-term cash deposits and a one-year fixed rate bond to cover these costs.

Her plan is to save regularly, over 15 years, to build up the substantial funds that will be required when there are two lots of higher education costs. In addition, there is a capital sum generously donated from her grandmother. These savings will ease the financial burden during what will then be an expensive time and the plan will achieve the goal of spreading the cost to avoid too much of an impact on her standard of living.

There is a limit to the monthly savings that can be made now, and Ruth recognises that investing everything into a low risk, low return fund (IL CERTS) will not provide sufficient returns to accumulate the capital that will be required. It is expected that the cost of university fees will rise at least in line with inflation and probably more.

Ruth is therefore prepared to invest 70% of the capital sum and her regular savings into an All Share index fund and 30% into IL CERTS.

Ruth accepts there will be periods when the stock market investment will show negative returns, but the mix of a growth fund and a low risk investment will mean that she will be able to tolerate the expected poor periods.

Her plan is to stop paying into stock market funds three years before the education costs start, and then to redirect the monthly savings to build up her cash deposits.

These cash deposits, and the IL CERTS, will pay for the fees in the early years. Ruth will never be put in a position where she is forced to sell the stock market fund, as there will be a planned exit.

At each yearly review the plan is to increase the monthly savings depending on Ruth's career progress and cost of living expenses.

Case study 3

The thoughtful grandmother

Elizabeth, Ruth's grandmother, is an 82-year-old widow in reasonable health, and like many of her age, she leads an active life. She had a successful career in local government and has her pension, and a good widow's pension. Both pensions are index-linked and these are more than sufficient for her needs.

With the help of her son Paul, she has put together a short written plan for her finances. Although she is concerned about the possible cost of care fees, should her health let her down in later life, her main goal was to leave her substantial savings to her son Paul and daughter Jill. As both are in a good financial position Paul suggested helping the four grandchildren. One of them, Ruth, is divorced and money is tight for her just now.

Elizabeth recognises that it will be more difficult for the young ones to provide for their own financial independence as their pension schemes will not be as good as hers, they will have big mortgages when they buy a house, and they are likely to have student loans to repay after completing their education.

Having done a few sums, Elizabeth realises she can afford to help Ruth and the others, and has given them all a capital sum to invest for her great-grandchildren.

This leaves her with an emergency fund invested with her local building society and a longer-term reserve, which she hopes will be inherited but it may be used to provide care fees.

Paul has said it is entirely reasonable to assume his mother Elizabeth could live to be 100 or more, and so her choice is to have the longer-term portfolio invested 45% into stock market funds and 55% in IL CERTS. In a really bad year she understands such a portfolio could be expected to fall about 15%, but more importantly, it would be expected to keep its head above water against long-term inflation.

Elisabeth considers herself to be a long-term investor, as she sees herself as the custodian of the family wealth, before it is passed down to the next generations. She may die young but the investments do not need to be sold on her death, as they can be split and then transferred to Paul and Jill.

Paul and Jill understand the plan. Following Elizabeth's death they intend to continue with the investments, which can be amended to fit their needs at that time.

Future reviews will consider the allocation of her money between the short-term and long-term and it is the intention to make further gifts in the future.

Case study 4
The late starters

Mark has always managed to keep employed during his career in sales, although he has never stayed in the same job for more than five years. Now that his children have flown the nest he and his wife Jean have reflected on their future.

For the first time they have sat down together to make a plan. They were prompted into action following the repayment of the mortgage – the expected lump sum from the maturity of the mortgage endowment policy did not materialise as expected.

Mark and Jean started the review process by checking their pension statements and they have come to realise that the original idea of retiring at 60 is out of the question. It is also unrealistic to expect to be able to save enough to fund what could turn out to be a very long retirement from age 65, as they do not have enough surplus income without the state pension, which will start in their late 60's.

Their existing savings in cash deposits are needed to cover all their possible short-term needs and emergencies.

Mark and Jean decide to save as much as they can for the longer-term but they no longer have a fixed retirement date and will review the situation as they go along. A main objective is not to be totally reliant on state benefits in their old age. At some date in the future they will reduce their working hours, moving towards retirement gradually and much later in life than they originally anticipated.

They decide to invest 60% into an international stock market fund and 40% into IL CERTS. They know that a higher percentage in stock markets will provide a better growth opportunity, but holding 40% of savings in secure funds limits the downside risk.

The first year review

WHEN AN investor has selected a 50/50 portfolio this decision is made to limit the investment risk. If stock markets subsequently have had a good run upwards, during a time when inflation is low, the portfolio will no longer be 50/50.

If it is left without a review, it could change to be 60/40 or 75/25 and although this is good news, because it means that money has been made, it also increases the exposure to risk compared to the original 50/50.

The action required is called a rebalancing, and it is a simple matter of re-adjusting the assets back to the original percentages.

The rebalancing advantage is not difficult to demonstrate. Over the 20 years to 2008, the worst year for a 50/50 portfolio, which was rebalanced annually, would have been minus 15%. If it had not been rebalanced, the worst year would have been minus 28.8%. This is quite a shock to the system if you had expected the worst year to be only half of this loss.

We know there is a chance of the first year showing a loss, and this is why we include IL CERTS, to control the downside risk. It could be that the portfolio which started as 50/50 could end the first year close to a 40% stock market and 60% IL CERTS.[9]

9 After a stock market fall the investor should rebalance. If there is no new cash entering the portfolio to implement rebalancing, it may be a good strategy to sell some IL CERTS to release the cash required. IL CERTS can be sold after the first anniversary. The investor benefits from index-linking although the interest rate above inflation may be reduced.

Rebalancing restores the stock market percentage, and when there is a recovery – it is certain there will be a recovery but we just don't know when – this will improve the investment return.

In effect you have introduced an annual routine, which is either selling some of your stock market investments after a good run, or buying stock market investments after a fall.

If there are periods when stock markets perform poorly for a few years in a row, initially the rebalancing will be detrimental, as it will lower the return. However, over the longer run the system will work well.

When to rebalance

The best time to rebalance is at each annual review or following the addition of a significant amount of capital. We can now go back to the case study first year reviews.

The review of Case study 1
The short-term investor

John had saved a few thousand pounds to pay for the family holiday. He invested his cash into an account that paid a bonus for the first six months with no catches. This foresight meant he had a good holiday and money to spare.

This year he decides to build up a reserve for a change of car in three years time, using the excess holiday cash to get started.

Although he likes the idea of IL CERTS, these would not be suitable if he were to change the car in two years time. The best option is to continue to use a good cash deposit account.

The review of Case study 2
The careful young parent

Ruth was prepared to invest 70% of her capital and regular savings into an All Share index fund and 30% into IL CERTS.

The first year was good for investing and as a result her portfolio is now 80% stock market and 20% IL CERTS. Her grandmother has gifted her a modest lump sum and using this to purchase more IL CERTS will bring the mix back to 70/30.

Ruth received an above average pay increase, well above inflation, and therefore she has increased her monthly savings.

The review of Case study 3
The thoughtful grandmother

Elizabeth decided to have her longer-term portfolio made up of 45% stock market funds and 55% in IL CERTS. The first year was good for investing and a decision was made to sell 5% of the stock market funds, to reinvest in IL CERTS, as this will bring the balance back to 45/55.

The review showed that too much had been set to one side for short-term needs and therefore modest capital sums were distributed to each of the grandchildren.

The review of Case study 4
The late starters

Mark and Jean started saving as much as they could for the longer-term. They decided to invest 60% into an international stock market fund and 40% into IL CERTS. After six months of investing, which was not good for them as all world stock markets were down over the period, Jean inherited £20,000 from a great aunt.

Mark and Jean are not discouraged and think it is good to be investing the unexpected inheritance after a stock market fall. They appreciate this is no indication of what the next 12 months will bring.

The new investing is done in such a way to bring the investments back to the preferred 60/40 mix.

SECTION 5
THE VALUE OF GOOD ADVICE

The value of good advice

"A certain amount of opposition is a great help to a man. Kites rise against, not with the wind."

—John Neill

THE VALUE of good advice can be explained in the context of an experience a friend of mine had when buying a plane ticket. He arranged to meet his son in New York but he was living in Chicago at the time. His point of arrival in America was JFK airport in New York and due to the travel arrangements he only needed to buy a one-way flight from New York to Chicago. He called a ticket agency and asked for the ticket.

As he arrived in Chicago, he had a conversation with another traveller who told him he had paid well over the odds for the flight, as the cost of a return flight was normally one quarter of what he had paid. Feeling cheated out of a few hundred dollars, he asked the ticket agency why he had been charged so much. The manager of the ticket agency said,

"Yes, you could have got a deal on a return flight, but you called and instructed us to buy a single ticket and a single ticket is much more expensive than a return ticket. This is a booking agency and not an advisory service." All his protests fell on deaf ears.

A good adviser will not just follow your instructions. Suggestions will be offered to improve your plan, and there will be times when they will challenge your assumptions.

You may think you have enough knowledge to make good financial decisions, but if there are complexities in your planning such as owning a business, having your own private pension fund, paying a lot of tax (and you wish to pay less), or one of your goals includes a wish to preserve your family wealth for future generations, you are unlikely to know all you need to know and you should take advice.

When a portfolio exceeds £250,000 it is also more likely you will benefit from professional advice as the DIY portfolios are good, but they will not work as well for larger portfolios and there are significant enhancements that can be engineered.

As we enter a period of higher than ever tax, the investment framework for a larger portfolio should be planned carefully, and this is probably something you should not tackle on our own. I think the stakes are too high without the right financial coach by your side.

For example, index strategies add an edge to self employed and corporate pension planning, but you do not want to buy the wrong ticket when it comes to an important element of a retirement strategy, and one which can impact on your NI liability, income tax, corporation tax, inheritance tax planning and the net investment return. Regretfully, effective tax planning[1] is more difficult than it was a few years ago.

---

1 An important part of any investment strategy is maximising the after-tax return. However, it is too easy to be seduced by expensive tax planning schemes, which reduce the tax bill for a year but then turn out to be poorly structured investments that lose money. Do not let the tax tail wag the investment dog.

How to spot the wrong adviser

WHEN YOU appreciate the advantages of an index strategy and you wish to find an adviser who can implement a plan for you, it is important to select a good adviser.

You should steer clear of any adviser who claims to be able to do any of the following:

- Identify the best fund managers, who can outperform the markets due to their forecasting skills.
- Spot the next big investment trend and get you in early with the promise of big profits.
- Tell you the best time to buy, and then the best time to sell before a market sector falls.

If there is talk of special discounts to reduce the cost of investing, or of rebates, then you are being offered expensive investments that pay commissions to advisers.

The adviser you are looking for will not be offering a choice between commissions and fees, as the quality index funds do not pay commissions, and therefore you should not expect free advice other than a meeting or two to establish if you can build a working relationship. Before agreeing to work together you will have agreed the basis of the fee for running your portfolio.

You must make sure the adviser is on the FSA's register of independent financial advisers and also has the experience to implement the strategy.[2]

> **How is your adviser paid?**
>
> Jack receives a call from his adviser. He is advised to carry out some changes to his portfolio. He asks a few questions and the answers seem both plausible and sensible, so he says he is happy to go ahead.
>
> Before he hangs up he thinks of a question. "How much are you going to charge me for this?" The reply: "As a good client you get a big discount, so we only charge 1%..." Or 2%...
>
> The more Jack runs up costs by chopping and changing his investments, the more his broker, adviser or bank earns out of him. Once he gets it into his head that this advice might be compromised, he decides to review the way he pays for advice.
>
> Suppose the reply was, "We make nothing extra Jack, it is all included in the fee you pay us every year for advising you." Isn't this better? The phone call is now costing the adviser time and money so you should only expect a call for the right reason.

Good planning can often be a little boring, and this can be reassuring. Why would you want surprises about poor

---

[2] A Chartered Financial Planner or a Certified Financial Planner is highly qualified although many are unfamiliar with the academic evidence surrounding index strategies. Also, many of them earn a living through commissions.

performance, or the excitement of big losses and sleepless nights because you did not understand how it all went wrong?

We can only take sporting analogies so far, but every successful sports team, Olympic champion and world gold medal winner has a coach or a team of experts at their disposal. No one ever succeeds without a good coach. When a team fails to succeed, it is usually the coach who gets the boot before any of the players. It is assumed that the players have underperformed due to a lack of sound guidance.

The successful DIY investor is a rare breed

"The solutions all are simple – after you have arrived at them. But they're simple only when you know already what they are."
—Robert M. Pirsig

I HAVE NEVER met any an amateur investor who has done well over the long run without some good financial coaching.

People need a smart financial coach, because they make just the same mistakes as the wrong type of adviser.

Look around, and it is not difficult to find people who are both intelligent and successful in their professions and businesses. The keys to investment success are not a secret, so why is it that so very few investors are equipped to run a successful portfolio, no matter how simple we can make it?

A high IQ is only one part of what most people would call smart. IQ measures only certain mental aptitudes – not the ability to make sound judgements – and IQ alone is a poor indicator of how good people will be at doing a particular job, such as investing.

Our brains have two systems to work out any given solution. One is intuitive and spontaneous and the other is the use of reasoning and deliberation to solve a problem. It is this spontaneous side that does not work well when our subconscious mind puts too much faith in our own perspective.

Nobel Prize winner Daniel Kahneman says intelligence is about brainpower, whereas rational thinking is about control. People with an IQ that is more than sufficient to run an investment portfolio often make the mistake of relying on their intuition. They can often rely on their intuition in their everyday life but they do not apply the right kind of thinking to an investing problem. Any investing knowledge and experience is easily overridden by inbuilt cognitive biases. Faced with a portfolio that is falling in value people often make an emotional decision, rather than a reasoned decision, on whether to buy, sell or hold.

When I am asked to briefly explain how a smart adviser can help a client, I would say it is to protect clients from themselves. A client can be their own worst enemy, and their adviser can stop them from making big mistakes.

When a client calls his adviser to say they are going to buy a bigger house and then cash in and live off the profits when they retire, or they are going to buy a ski chalet in Bulgaria off-plan because everyone else is doing it, the adviser can stop them.

If the client is thinking of selling their investments because recently stock markets have been falling and everyone says the outlook is bad, the adviser can tell them that this is a bad idea. A quick reality check can be priceless.

Acting on Sunspots

'Sunspots' is a term used by Economists to describe news or events that should not influence markets but often do when enough people believe they will. The name comes from a 19th century English economist who suggested that sunspot activity could be the cause of economic cycles. Identifying sunspots from real news is often difficult as we often disagree over what might be important.

For example, a newspaper article recommending a number of stocks can be a sunspot, although it should not be when it only represents the author's opinion and contains nothing new. However, if people act on the advice in numbers, the price of the named stocks may change in line with the prediction, and it can become self-fulfilling (at least for a while).

When the Chancellor speaks in Parliament or officials at the Bank of England issue a statement, they must be aware of sunspots. Vague announcements seem to work very well, because it is hard to speculate about an official statement when you are bamboozled by it.

An adviser can do more than stop you making big mistakes, of course. You should expect help with your financial plan, and a review of elements that you may not have considered sufficiently, or overlooked. Upon closer examination, your main goals may not be achievable without a U-turn, or they might be simply unrealistic.

More advanced investment strategies

THERE ARE now more sophisticated investment strategies available to the professional index investor that the DIY investor cannot access.

I have spent some time explaining why it is good to base your growth investments on the FTSE All Share index and international index funds. Having said this, there are significant improvements that can be made to the basic portfolio, with the prospect of a better return or less volatility.

The FTSE All Share index was designed as a tool to measure the ups and downs of the UK stock market, and to serve as a benchmark for professionals wishing to compare different strategies and managers. Although it represents 98% of the UK market and over 600 individual shareholdings, the top 10 FTSE shares account for nearly half of the entire index.

BP and Shell make up well over 20% of the index. The result is that your fortunes will often depend on the results of a few enormous companies. If you invest £1,000 in an FTSE All Share index fund over £200 will be in BP and Shell, and £300 will be divided between another 8 shares.

This problem has led to the development of bespoke indices that limit the amount that can be held in any one stock. This in turn allows an increase in the weighting of the middle ranking and smaller companies. The advantage is greater diversity and the likelihood of improved returns over time.

Low cost bespoke index solutions, available to fee-based advisers, allow the construction of portfolios that include a Value Index, emerging market index and Small Company Index funds. Academic evidence demonstrates that such strategies add diversity, reduce volatility and improve investor returns over the long run.

Two index providers, Dimensional and Vanguard, have made the same decision. They have made their funds available to fee-only advisers, but not to commission-based advisers. I think both of them recognise the impartiality of fee-based professionals. Others might argue it is down to limited resources; making it impractical for them to deal directly with a general public that often needs to be educated. However, such considerations never stopped other sales-oriented fund management groups from distributing every investment idea that was marketable.

Investing in Value and small companies

Imagine for a moment that the stock market has two extremes. At one end of the spectrum, investors invest in companies that are familiar. They feel that they understand these businesses, and how they trade and make profits. They are confident these companies will continue to be successful in the future.

At the other end of the spectrum, investors tend to shy away from investing in stocks that are unfamiliar. People do not understand how they make their profits. It could be that investors are not certain about their future, and they may have made losses recently, or received unfavourable reviews in the press.

Because the established companies are held in high regard,

there is a good demand for their shares, and as a result the prices are high. The price of these favourites will not go significantly higher unless they have an even better story to tell or some exceptional trading results.

Unfamiliar companies are not held in high regard because they are seen as higher risk. The only way a sensible investor could be tempted to buy them is if the share price is low enough to compensate for the risk. In other words there is an opportunity to make a higher return. If you invest in such companies, you are 'value investing'.

Such a company may announce a poor trading result, but if it is not as bad as the market expected, or the trading strategy becomes understood over time, the price will go up and more interest is created. Sometimes the fortunes of a value stock can improve significantly simply because it comes to be viewed less pessimistically.

Over the long term, introducing index funds that invest only in value stocks will enhance a portfolio, but not in each and every year.[3] There can be a run of years when value companies underperform the main market indices. But this is what you should expect, because if value shares always outperformed the main market there would be no risk.

Introducing a small company index fund will also improve matters, but the results are not as reliable as the 'value premium'. Small companies are charged more when they want to raise capital, as they are generally a higher risk than their larger counterparts. Diversification is the key – some small companies will fair badly but others may have spectacular success.

3 This is not a universally accepted observation. There are a number of academics and practitioners who do not accept the value premium exists and the returns of value stocks are linked to the economic and credit cycle.

The cost of trading can be a problem when investing in small companies, as there is a big difference between the cost price and the selling price of small stocks. People who manage their own share portfolios often do not realise just how tough trading in small companies can be until they experience the high costs for themselves.

For success with small companies, the best professionals will employ a smart trading strategy built on patience, buying shares where large trades are done by negotiation, and the fund manager is not bound by a strict indexing policy.

UK value and small company investing 20-years to 2008

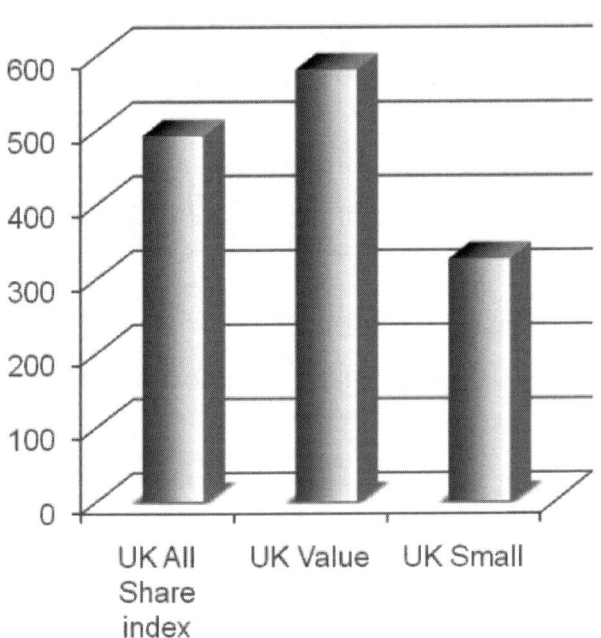

Global value and small companies

The principles of investing in value companies and small companies works equally well when investing in overseas markets.

Global investing 20-years to 2008

Total growth % 1988–2008

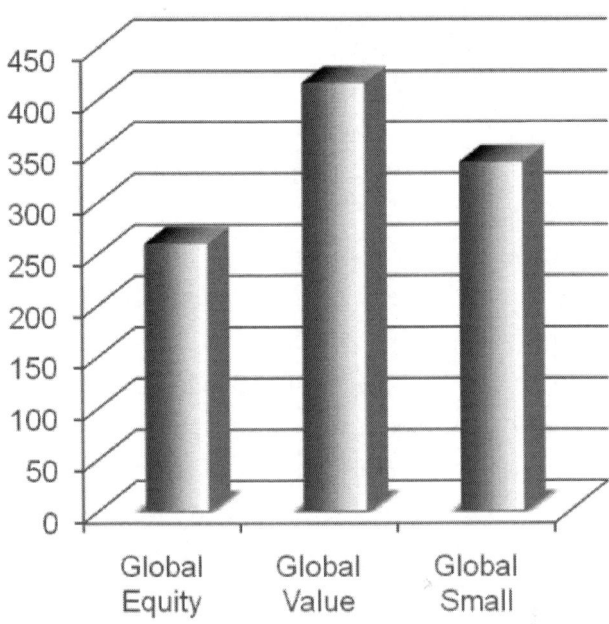

Defensive investing

In the DIY portfolio I recommended ILNS Certificates as a defensive investment, because they are easy to understand and easy to buy. However, building a truly defensive investment portfolio is usually quite difficult.

You won't go far wrong in picking National Savings Certificates, but for a larger portfolio they are often inconvenient and unlikely to offer the best solution. In a large portfolio, even if sufficient ILNS Certificates could be made available, there would be no diversity. For example, during a long period of low inflation, the returns on index-linked bonds may be less than traditional fixed rate bonds. Over the last 20 years the return on ILNS certificates has been about one percent a year less than one month T-Bills.

If we set to one side the toxic investments, which are misleadingly held out to be defensive, investors should be buying low risk government and corporate bonds. In a world of active management far too many bond funds are presented as low risk investments, when in fact they can be quite volatile.

Part of the problem is that active managers must overcome their own high fees, so there is something left over for the investor. The only answer is to invest in higher risk bonds. Often, the managers succeed in their objective, which is to satisfy the investor with a return above the deposit rate. However, there have been many occasions when this kind of strategy fails, and the investors suffer an unexpected loss.

The past performance of funds promoted as defensive, which invest actively in gilts and bonds, is of no value in helping an investor to choose a suitable investment.

Gilts and bonds behave in a similar way to stock markets as they are both in 'forward thinking' markets. If the majority of investors believe interest rates or the rate of inflation will be going up or down, they will buy speculatively to try to outperform the market.

When there is a change to the Bank of England base rate, or to the rate of inflation, the markets may not move much at all. This is because many investors have anticipated a change and will have already made their move. However, if the investors are wrong footed, because the forecast or presumption they acted on was wrong, they stand to lose money. They will stand to lose a lot of money if they own the 'wrong' type of bond.

Long-dated bonds and gilts are volatile when interest rates change. If interest rates and inflation fall, the investor can make very good returns, but this is missing the point. Bear in mind that the original intention was one of safety. If interest rates and inflation unexpectedly increase, against the general consensus view, the holders of long-dated bonds often get clobbered.

The key to defensive investing is to ensure you are not exposed to shocks in the market. This can only be achieved by owning corporate bonds of high quality, and gilts and corporate bonds that are not likely to suffer when interest rates change. Defensive funds make low returns, as this is the trade-off for safety.

APPENDICES

Buying your own index investment funds

WHEN YOU choose a fund there are only three things you need to know. The fund strategy and how it replicates the index it is tracking, how successful has it been at doing its job, and the cost.

You should buy a fund that tracks *either* the FTSE All Share index, *or* a global index such as the MSCI World index or one of the FT global indices (the fund description will say if the UK market is included or excluded).

It is important to ensure that the method used by your fund to track the index is a good one. Your fund should aim to replicate the index. Replication is when the fund physically owns each of the stocks in the index. Be wary of funds that also use 'sampling' as a method of tracking an index.

Sampling, in my view, should only be acceptable when it is used as a method to lower trading costs. The result is a reduction in the number of stocks that carry little weight in the index. A genuine tracking fund will physically buy all of the stocks required to accurately track the index.

Fund success

Unlike actively managed funds, where past performance is erroneously used to infer management skill, the past performance of a tracker fund is useful. You can review the history of a fund to check if the method of tracking used has successfully mirrored the chosen index.

An index fund should be able to track an index exactly with full replication, have less cost than an actively managed fund, and have only a relatively small margin of error due to sampling. For example, if an index is up or down 5% in a year, the fund you are researching should match the index return of 5%, less the annual charges, plus or minus a small margin for tracking error.

Tracking error due to sampling can be advantageous, although it is good to remember that an advantageous tracking error could prove to be detrimental in the long run.

For example, if the index is up 9% and the costs of the fund are 1%, then you should expect the performance to be very close to 8%. If the return was actually 9%, because the 1% tracking error was favourable during this particular period, the next year could just as easily return 1% less than expected. Tracking error on this scale should be avoided as such a fund is too volatile. There is no realistic prospect of a reward for this extra risk over time.

Expenses and costs

This can be the most difficult area to check out, as the information is not readily available unless you ask for it.

First of all, you should not expect to pay any upfront costs of any kind, other than a modest administration fee. In the actively managed fund sector it is not unusual to see an initial charge of 5%. When buying an index fund a 1% charge is far too much.

For the yearly costs, the most commonly quoted figure is the annual management charge (AMC) but this is only the charge made by the fund manager, and not the total cost of running the fund.

You must find out the 'Total Expense Ratio', or TER. To demonstrate the point, one fund management group has advertised the cost of a market leading index fund with an AMC of only 0.1%, but the TER was 0.3% the last time I looked. 0.3% is not bad if it is all there is to pay, but to advertise 0.1% is misleading.

If the sales people tell you the TER is not readily available you can tell them it will be found in the 'simplified prospectus' that firms must provide on request. Surprisingly, the TER is not the sum total of all costs, and for those who buy actively managed funds there would be a fair amount of additional research to do. However, for the index fund buyer, these additional costs should be very small.

A good piece of advice is to only invest in the things you know something about. Far too often, people make the mistake of believing hot tips, or act on something they read in a newspaper or a magazine.

The way to get rich slowly is to stick to what you know and trust. With index investing, it is possible to achieve success with a moderate amount of research.

Bear in mind that people rarely get rich by investing in things they know nothing about.

Employer pension schemes

More of us have an opportunity to decide how our pension scheme contributions are invested. This is due to the phasing out of Final Salary schemes, in favour of Money Purchase schemes. In the future, most of us will have a pension income determined by two factors.

- the size of the pension fund that can be built up
- annuity rates at the time of retirement

There is not much you can do to change or influence the annuity rate[1], but the final size of your pension pot will be determined by the total contributions, how long they are invested for and the rate at which these contributions grow. So, investing early is an advantage, and the investment performance will be a significant part of the equation.

It is generally good advice to join an employer's pension scheme. The employer makes a contribution, a percentage of your salary, and you are usually requested to make a contribution of your own. For example, an employer may offer to make a contribution of 5% of your pay and you are expected to contribute 3% or 5% of your pay. It would usually be unwise to refuse such an offer because you are being given a tax-efficient pay rise.

The majority of pension scheme members will make the mistake of not getting involved in the investment process and

---

1 There may be other options at retirement, including an 'Unsecured Income', although the income that can be arranged is linked to the prevailing annuity rate.

their contributions will be invested into the 'default fund' suggested by the scheme's adviser. This will be a Managed Fund with a broad spread of stock market, gilt, corporate bond and property fund investments.

There will often be a better option, which is to invest into an index fund. This should be the basis of your fund choice and you can build your pension portfolio in a similar way to that described earlier.

When you are looking for a defensive fund, to complement the equity tracker fund, you will not have the option to buy ILNS Certificates. As an alternative, you should look for a fund investing into short-dated corporate bonds, or short-dated gilts, or index-linked gilts or a combination of these. However, the important characteristic is to choose a fund that is not going to be volatile. Its purpose is to cushion the blow during times of stock market trauma.

If there is no index option, this should not deter you from joining the scheme, providing the employer is making a good contribution. You will not have your preferred index investment, but you will have the employer's contribution to compensate you for not having a reliable investment choice (compared to index funds). However, it would be reasonable to ask your employer if it is possible to offer an indexing option. If the employer is installing a new scheme and there is no index fund it would be reasonable to ask for one to be included.

The Child Trust Fund

It is not often you receive a letter from HMRC that brings good news. However, the mother of every child born will receive a pack detailing the minimum £250 voucher available for their newborn son or daughter. A further payment of £250 is paid on their seventh birthday, and although the scheme is not perfect, parents should not 'look a gift horse in the mouth'.

£500 is certainly a good foundation to build savings for a child's future and a parent should be involved in the investment choice. The information booklet parents receive is headed 'What will yours grow into?' This is a good question, and although we do not know the answer, we do know the growth will be determined by the investment choice. For example, over eighteen years, the evidence suggests that investing into cash deposits is unlikely to offer the best return.

There are a number of approved investment providers offering the option of an index fund. Index fund options are offered through stakeholder accounts, which have a maximum charge of 1.5% for the first 10 years and 1.0% thereafter. There are other index choices through share accounts (non-stakeholder).

Many parents will use the gift from the Government as a foundation for a savings scheme and wish to make their own contributions. My advice is not to make your own contributions through the Child Trust Fund for two reasons. The first is that you are likely to find an index fund of your own choice with a lower charging structure than 1.5%, which is the stakeholder charge over the first 10 years. The second reason is a practical one; a parent should wish to keep control, and not give the child the option to go and spend all those savings following their 18th birthday.

It is harder than you think to beat the average return

WHEN WE talk about the average return for a stock market investor, the number we seek is what a statistician would call the mean. The statistical mean is not as useful as the statistical mode, which is the most likely occurrence in a sample.

Imagine a Post Office queue of ten people, not an unfamiliar sight in my town, and we are told the average wealth of the queue is £500,000. This statistic is misleading because nine people in the queue have savings of £5,000 between them and one of them is a multimillionaire.

None of the nine non-millionaires in the queue will feel any richer because the average wealth is £500,000. In this kind of scenario it is better to use the mode, because it measures the most commonly occurring figure rather than the average. If you pick somebody at random from the queue, it will most likely be one the nine representing the statistical mode, the most common occurrence in this sample.

This is relevant when studying stock market returns, because the most common experience for investors is an investment return that is below the average. The average return is usually inflated by the few shares that perform much better than most of the other shares during any given period.

IT IS HARDER THAN YOU THINK TO BEAT THE AVERAGE RETURN

This has important consequences for those who only buy their favourite shares instead of all the shares available. Although they may be lucky and select shares that outperform the market, the odds are against them, and most active investors will underperform the stock market index and experience a below average investment return.

There is research to show that if you are unable to pick the top 25% of stocks each year, you are unlikely to earn any profit at all. This is quite a challenge for those who think they might be good at picking shares, because whenever they pick a favourite company stock there is only a 1 in 4 chance it will be among the winners.

The same principle applies when talking chances with Premium Bond investing, and buying National Lottery tickets. The very few big winners take the lion's share from the rest.

From November 2008, the odds of winning in the monthly Premium Bond draw were stretched out to 1 in 36,000. Of the prizes handed out by Premium Bonds, over 97 out of every 100 prizes was £50, while an almost insignificant 24 prizes in a million exceeded £1,000. There is a bias towards small prizes, so almost all of the prize money goes to £50 or £100 winners.

There are a few people who do well out of Premium Bonds by winning a £1 million. Of course, it is the thought of the big win that gives us the incentive to buy them, but the real winners are few and far between. Premium Bonds are essentially a form of gambling and they offer very poor odds.

Reducing volatility is important

There was a time when everyone was happy to measure fund performance with a simple benchmark.[1] In the modern world this is not good enough and quite rightly there are also measures of volatility.[2]

By measuring volatility, we can expose the fund manager who is temporarily out-performing the market by taking on more risk. If a fund manager slightly out-performs a well-known benchmark such as the FTSE 100 index, but exposes the investors to double the volatility, then this is not a good fund management strategy, because it can have a detrimental effect on investment returns.

Here is a simple illustration to demonstrate the point. The first row is a hypothetical performance for £100,000 invested in the FTSE All-Share index. In the first year the market is down by 10%, and in the second year it goes back up by 10%. The investment is worth £99,000 at the end.

	1st year return	2nd year return	Average Return	Compound Return	Value at the end of 2nd year
Index fund	-10%	+10%	0%	-0.5%	£99,000
Active fund 1	-20%	+22%	1%	-3.0%	£97,000
Active fund 2	-50%	+50%	0%	-13.4%	£75,000

1 In the investment world benchmarking is a standard by which fund management performance can be measured or judged against the competition
2 A common measure of volatility is the Sharpe Ratio, devised by a Nobel prize-winning economist. It examines the relationship between investment returns and their volatility.

The second and third rows are actively managed funds that are more volatile than the FTSE All-Share index. The end result is not as good although the average returns are equal to or better than the index fund.

Volatility is an important factor, because it can have the effect of producing an inferior return.

The tax-free ISA allowance

IT IS important to make use of all available tax allowances and tax breaks to increase your net investment return. After all, it is the net return after tax, that you can actually spend.

At the time of writing the simplest tax break is the ISA allowance. Cash can be invested into an ISA every year, and if the allowance is not used it is lost. There is a higher ISA allowance for investing into stocks and shares and bonds.

I am often asked if the allowance should be used for cash deposits or stocks and bonds. As you should aim to preserve your tax-free investments, then whenever it is appropriate, your ISA allowance should be used for your long-term stock market and bond investments.

The industry's poor record of treating customers fairly

The insurance and investment industry has never had a great track record when it comes to 'treating its customers fairly'.

EVERYONE OVER the age of 35 will have heard of 'the man from the Pru'. It wasn't always just the Pru, of course, but also the Pearl, Liverpool Victoria (now rebranded LV) and Refuge and so on. At one time there was a legion of salesmen who came to your door to collect the premiums for regular savings plans.

They disappeared from the scene very quickly, and the industry said it was because it was no longer cost effective to collect door-to-door. The real reason is that new regulations were introduced that exposed very high charges, and these door-to-door policies became an embarrassment.

Policies would often have to earn an investment return of over 9% a year, to cover policy charges.

Low cost Stakeholder investments

The Government has made a real effort to reduce the cost of investing. It introduced what were called 'stakeholder' products. Standards were set for low-cost savings and pensions, with a maximum charge of 1% a year and no catches, but they never caught on because the industry largely avoided selling them.

Stakeholder contracts did not suit the industry's sales driven culture because it was not possible to accommodate a high rate of commission for the salespeople.

Amazingly, a number of large insurance companies went along with the Government at the beginning and introduced stakeholder products. For them though, it was an act of madness, because the insurers then had to admit they would be running stakeholder products at a loss for years. Also, they were cutting off their lifeline to new business, as they could not reward supporting sales teams with the high commissions they demanded.

They were always going to have to surrender to the demand for more commission, and they did.

The price of stakeholder products was allowed to increase, but they have failed to sell in significant numbers compared to the sales of other more expensive products.

The most common toxic investments

"It is often said that men are ruled by their imaginations; but it would be truer to say they are governed by the weakness of their imaginations."

—Walter Bagehot

THIS SECTION discusses the problems investors are likely to encounter with the following investments:

- With-profit funds
- Property funds
- Guaranteed stock market investments
- Hedge funds
- Venture Capital trusts and other tax saving schemes
- Fund of funds

With-profit funds

"FSA research found that when smoothing was explained to consumers as a process whereby providers held back and redelivered returns at their discretion, they did not find this an attractive concept." Sandler Review, 2002

In 1762 Equitable Life was born and it invented modern life insurance. By 1781 it was distributing bonuses to policyholders, and so the with-profit system was born.

By 2007 about £400 billion was invested in with-profit funds through life insurance endowments, personal pensions and single premium bonds. Single premium bonds started about 20 years ago as a way of investing in the stock market with the insurance company taking the short-term risks. The idea of a smooth investment return linked to the prosperity of the stock market has great appeal to investors. It is also a unique selling proposition and hence the big sales numbers.

With-profit bonds earned a lot of commission for sales teams, who promised investors a no-risk investment that yielded high returns and annual bonuses that could be taken as an annual income. Unfortunately, very few customers bothered to look beyond the glittering veneer to examine how these investment funds are actually managed.

During the tech bubble high bonuses were maintained in a time when all insurance company assets were collapsing. As long ago as August 2000, the Faculty and Institute of Actuaries wrote to its members to advise there was a mismatch between the bonuses and the reserves set aside by the life assurance companies to underpin their future liabilities. Regardless of this the Prudential, which holds about 25% of the entire with-profit market, continued to promote with-profit funds as a safe haven for investors.[1] Many investors were vulnerable to with-profit propaganda because of declining deposit rates, which plunged from about 10% to 4% between 1992 and the year 2000. Investors were desperate for low-risk income, but the reality is that with-profit bonds have never been as safe as some experts have claimed them to be.

1 Gavin Stewart, the retail marketing director at the Pru said at the time: "They aren't necessarily as exciting as unit trusts but you won't lose sleep over them."

The prospects for those who invested in with-profit funds remain bleak. Anybody who wishes to get out of their with-profit funds should always take advice before surrendering a policy, and there are a number of specialist firms offering an evaluation service.

There is additional complexity when evaluating the value of an endowment policy linked to a with-profit fund because you must take into account the loss of any life insurance cover

One area of confusion is the facility to withdraw 5% a year from a With Profit Bond without having to account for the income on a tax return. It should be understood that this is a deferment, and not a tax-free situation. Also, if the investor withdraws the 5% income, and the annual bonuses are less than 5%, then the fund is reducing in value every year.

Property funds

Investing in property has long been regarded as a formula for investment success hence the phrase, 'as safe as houses'. Most managed funds invest in commercial property, shops and offices and the value of a fund is often determined by the value of the rental income.

Most existing property funds were sold at a time when investors had forgotten that property prices can go down as well as up, and fund managers encouraged the idea that property was a one-way bet. Towards the end of what could be described as the great property bubble – a global phenomenon – investors were falling over themselves to buy property in Spain and ski chalets in Bulgaria on the basis of a few drawings and a glossy brochure.

A great selling point for a property bond was the concept

that property prices rise in a smooth and constant manner (rather like the magical with-profit fund), and you can draw up to 5% a year income net of tax (the same tax structure as a with-profit bond) with no tax to declare at the time.

The question to ask is 'Where is this absence of volatility coming from and how is it achieved?'

Property funds can be valued to suit the whims of the fund manager. Every month, a valuer estimates the value of the buildings in a property fund. This valuation is essentially a guess, as the true value of a property can only be known when there is an agreed sale on the property.

For a moment let's be cynical. Suppose a valuer estimates a property fund to have increased in value by 5% since the last valuation. Why not say the property has only gone up by 2%? This is enough good news for the investors, as they will be happy with the prospect of a rate equivalent to a 24% return a year (2% x twelve months). However, it may be in the fund manager's interests to under value the fund as it leaves room for manoeuvre. If the following month the property has gone down by 2%, there is still '3% to play with' from the previous month. The fund can then show a one percent increase to keep both the investors and the marketing manager happy. During the good months 'a reserve' can be built up for a rainy day, and the fund shows no volatility.

The marketing literature can paint a picture of a very steady investment return, with no downturns. This works until the property value does take a real turn for the worse, and then the whole lot implodes.

Selling property during a downturn can be very difficult. If it is known the manager has to sell property because everyone wants to get out of the fund, the asking price will quickly collapse. Other property funds will be suffering in the same way and trying to sell property to pay off investors. The actual value in these circumstances will be very different to the mythical valuations given in rosier economic times.

If a commercial property has no tenants, then there will be a negative cash flow because of the cost of maintaining and insuring the property.

Many property funds are beefed up with bank loans in an effort to improve returns. For example, a property fund might invest £50 million, and borrow a further £50 million at 5% interest to buy a total of £100 million worth of property. This is brilliant if the value of the fund is going up at the rate of 10% a year.

Unfortunately, if the property halves in value, and there are plenty of examples of this happening, there is nothing left at all for anyone, except an outstanding debt owed to the bank.

When property funds go wrong, they go horribly wrong, and in many cases you just cannot get your money back. The managers impose a moratorium, meaning you will be given an opportunity to withdraw from the fund later on when they manage to sell the property.

Do not buy a property fund without professional advice and a full understanding of the risks involved. Could the investment halve in value? Could the investment collapse? Find out and get it in writing before you buy.

Property funds are expensive and too many investors buy them on a speculative basis. The nature of property is such that it is not liquid enough to cope with wild swings in short term investor demand.

Property can be a good long-term investment but it seems there will never be any retail property funds available at low cost and they will never be able to replicate any of the property indices.

Most investors would be better to ignore property funds unless they are prepared to take professional advice.

> **Buy-to-let gearing**
>
> People who borrow money for buy-to-let property are attracted by the idea of 'gearing up'.
>
> Consider a 90% mortgage on a £200,000 buy-to-let property. At first there is a £200,000 investment for an initial deposit of £20,000. The cheap mortgage deal means that there is an income for the landlord as the tenant's rent is higher than the monthly mortgage, and it seems like a great idea.
>
> Suppose the property falls 20% in value. The investor is now stuck with negative equity, because the property is worth less than the mortgage. If interest rates go up, so there is insufficient rent to cover the mortgage, then there is a cash flow problem. If there is no tenant, there is an even bigger big cash flow problem.
>
> If you were advised to take out a big loan to buy stocks and shares, most people would say that you were investing foolishly. For some reason, speculative borrowing to buy a property is acceptable.

Guaranteed stock market investments

These are also called Guaranteed Equity Bonds (GEB's). The advertisement below is typical for this kind of investment. The danger is that the stock market could fall during the investment term and trigger a loss at maturity.

Some of these investments are designed for growth, but if the stock market falls below a certain level, there is no profit and there could be a loss of your capital.

> ## The Opportunity for Annual or Monthly Regular Income
>
> This Regular Income Bond is designed to bridge the gap between low risk/low return deposits and high income/high risk investments. The Bond is a five-year investment where investors receive a regular income. There is a choice of either a monthly or an annual income option.
>
> Annual Income Option – 7.6% or
>
> Monthly Income Option – 0.62%
>
> Capital at Risk Investment*
>
> Investment Term – 5 Years
>
> *The return of your capital depends on the performance of the FTSE 100 Index and the ability of the counterparty to repay the monies.

When we do invest in the stock market the profit comes from two different sources. The first is the expected long-term capital growth, and the second is a flow of dividend income. These products do not offer the second part – you do not get the five years of dividends representing about 15% or 20% of your original investment. This is an expensive guarantee.

But with all of these investments the guarantee depends on the ability of a third party to secure the scheme, called the 'counter-party'. Too many of these investments have failed because the counter-party went bust.[2]

GEB's are often in a package with a term deposit account. For example, offering a 5% fixed rate on one half of the investment for 12 months (when the best going rate is 2.5%), and half the money going into a GEB. For these to work it is a simple matter of the very profitable GEB subsiding the fixed rate.

A much better alternative for a cautious investor would be to put a small percentage of their investment into an index tracker and the rest into a National Savings Certificate.

Hedge funds

The idea of hedging started with land in the 16th century. Impenetrable spiky hawthorns were used in hedges to limit the size of a field, to secure it and limit the risk.

The phrase 'Hedging your bets' now refers to the attempt of a gambler to spread the risk by not committing himself to only one possible outcome.

Hedge funds – also called Absolute Return Funds – are popular, taking their name from the old methods of limiting risk except they often do the exact opposite. They take high

---

2 Structured products that have failed include those offered by Eurolife and Key Data. Lehmans, the failed bank was the counter-party providing the guarantees built into structured products from L&G, and L&G was criticised for waiting four months before informing investors of the problem. Affected consumers will not be able to make a claim to the Financial Services Compensation Scheme, because the failure of Lehmans was an investment risk

risks, through a series of bets, they promise the earth and they fail often.

In 2006, only one in six hedge funds had a successful outcome and since then the failure rate has increased. Many hedge funds will have failed during the credit crunch because they were following a simple strategy of borrowing and buying high-risk assets which worked when the markets were going up. This is hardly a sophisticated strategy. In principle it is the same as buy-to-let, the difference being that risky stocks are favoured rather than property.

Hedge fund costs and failures

The idea of hedge fund management must have a very strong appeal to some investors. Why else would they be prepared to pay an annual fee of 2%, and 20% of any profit?

The managers tell you they make money whether stock markets go up or down, and this is the compelling proposition offered by Hedge Funds.

The big news at the beginning of 2008 was the collapse of the London based Peloton Hedge fund, which lost billions of investors' money. Peloton was named after the arrowhead shaped pack that forms behind the leader in a bicycle race, but its collapse represents more than a few buckled wheels.

Hedge funds have been around since the 1950's in the United States, and the idea of hedging was originally developed as a method of reducing risk, as in 'hedging your bets'. However, hedge fund managers have often got into in all sorts of difficult-to-explain activities trying to make massive gains.

These activities include 'short-selling', which is selling something you do not own in the hope the value will go down before you have to settle, and 'leverage' which is borrowing to invest so that profits (and losses!) are multiplied.

Hedge funds have acquired a reputation for secrecy, and certainly until recently, the regulatory regime that applied did not require a Hedge fund to make public too much information about its activities, and therefore not having to divulge trading activities.

Who would want to invest in a fund they do not understand, and have no idea of the risk involved for their capital? A significant number of formerly wealthy individuals did. Peloton shot to fame by raising almost $1 billion at launch, helped by the background of the partners who were former stars at Goldman Sachs.[3] They started to hit the jackpot in 2007. The original multi-strategy fund returned over 27% that year, while the ABS fund, made 86% and new money flooded in.

Peloton's ABS fund won the best new fixed income hedge fund award in January 2008, following its 86% gain, so the wind-up of the firm should remind professional fund managers about the dangers of borrowing to invest. When things go wrong they go spectacularly wrong. The fund could get completely wiped out, which is what happened in this case.

The global hedge fund industry had one of its worst months in January 2008, and according to hedge fund research the sector returned minus 1.8%. This figure was ridiculous, as it excluded losses of 50% and more for the worst performing funds. The problem is that they remove the failures so they only show the results of the survivors.

---

3 Outside the financial world they were best known as the victims of the personal assistant who was convicted of stealing $4.3 million from her bosses at Goldman Sachs. Her bosses had that much loose change they didn't notice the loss for a while.

Imagine a scenario. A hedge fund manager sends information to potential investors. One of them, Jane, takes notice of his great fund performance. The manager confirms that there is an opportunity to invest in a select fund for the privileged few, but the minimum investment is very high.

He tells her the fund is sure to outperform stock markets because he has a system that can reliably identify future winning strategies in advance. These may involve borrowing and buying heavily into markets to gear up the return, selling stocks he does not own to buy them back later when the share price has fallen, small unknown companies that will boom, interest rate bets, currency speculation and commodities trading.

His successful trading record proves that his uncannily good predictions give a performance better than any market return.

Jane tells all her friends, and they invest £50 million between them.

The money is not stolen; it is invested legitimately within the rules set by the FSA, and the investors are told that they are making a focused high-risk investment. Why should the investors care about the risk when the expert is always correct? The expert is very well paid as he takes a 6% starting commission – £3 million – and the money he will earn in the future is 20% of all the profits.

In fact he has no idea what the future holds but he makes a number of guesses, which turn out to be right, and everyone is ecstatic. He takes 20% of the profit. But then, as he expects will happen sometime, he gets it all wrong. Initially, every investor stays with the fund, but it is not long before Jane experiences heavy losses and ruin.

> Our expert could not care less as he pockets his millions and starts again.
> The unbeatable system did not really exist. The expert had a few 'seed' funds running concurrently, each trying different market bets, over the previous six months. As each month progressed, one or two failed and one or two looked very good. The expert had no idea which fund would win each month – it was simply a game of making different bets. The surviving fund was very marketable because the other fund failures were not discussed and they were simply erased.
> This is my interpretation of how the hedge fund industry works. The concept of 'seed funds' is not exclusive to the hedge fund industry, but a technique that has been employed by many in the fund management industry to market their funds.

Venture Capital trusts and other tax saving schemes

Venture Capital Trust (VCT) schemes started on 6 April 1995 and they were designed to encourage individuals to invest into small, higher-risk trading companies. The failure rate of these funds is high, so to encourage investors the Government offers tax incentives.

Investors will often be attracted by a tax saving, but there is not much point investing into something to save tax if the chance of getting your money back is slim.

Companies such as Shell, Barclays Bank or Marks & Spencer are quoted on the stock market. You can see the price of these stocks minute by minute. On the other hand, the small companies that are the main territory of VCT's, are not quoted.

An unquoted share can be valued on the basis of the last trade between an independent buyer and seller. Generally, as there are no such transactions, the value of the VCT stocks is no more than a guess.

It should not be too difficult to see how a problem can arise when the fund manager is looking for new customers. He can decide what valuation to use to make the fund performance look brilliant. As long as everyone is happy to stay invested, and experience what appears to be an ever-increasing value, there is no problem.

The investor's nightmare starts when a number of investors wish to make an exit, and when the VCT manager has to sell stocks to raise cash, they are found to have little value. This has happened all too frequently in the industry.

The investors do initially have the joy of tax relief but this is often followed by plenty of time to repent at leisure.

Fund of funds

These are something of a paradox. Although every active fund manager claims to be the best, it is not possible to identify a good one in advance as there are so few good ones.

To save you the trouble of hunting them down, a fund management group will offer a packaged off-the-shelf portfolio. The portfolio will be made up of some of its own in-house funds and also what it considers to be the best of the other fund managers (the competition).

There is a breakdown in logic somewhere down the line. Consider a fund management group running a European equity fund, an American equity fund and an Emerging Markets equity fund. However, in its fund-of-funds package these three geographical areas are managed by three of its competitors. This suggests either that the competition is running better funds than its own funds (in which case it should not be offering these inferior funds to the public), or that the investor ends up in some second-rate funds to fit in with the concept of a fund of funds product.

It cannot be a point of consumer choice, because the concept of fund-of-funds is that it takes an expert to pick funds, and the job is too difficult for the layperson.

Either way it's a poor idea, because the investor is paying a fund manager to recommend other highly paid fund managers. Somewhere, obscured and brushed aside in the detail, is the undeniable fact of there being two sets of charges. Investors must pay the fund of fund manager and also the fees of the third party fund managers.

These fund of funds are popular with commission earning advisers as they can be sold as one convenient package. The premise is that of having a broadly diversified portfolio, run by the best fund managers, with one of the best fund managers choosing the rest of them.

Regretfully, very little evidence exists to support the idea that a fund manager is good at picking other fund managers. For example, many of them selected New Star as a third-party manager before it was taken over. Going back to 2006 an article in the Observer[4] said, "There is now a wide range of these products to choose from, but those from New Star and Jupiter have the best track record and are well-regarded managers." New Star, as we know, turned out to be a disaster.

4 Written by Heather Connon in the Observer 18th June 2006

Reliable information comes from the academic world

1935 – 1950's	Analyse securities one by one, focus on picking winners and concentrate holdings to maximise returns. The conventional wisdom was that diversification was undesirable. At most three or four securities should be bought, as competent investors will never be satisfied beating the averages by a few small percentage points.
1962	**Harry Markowitz Nobel Prize in Economics, 1990** Diversification reduces risk. Assets should be evaluated by their effect on a portfolio and not by individual characteristics. An optimal portfolio can be constructed to maximise return for a given standard deviation.
1965	**Paul Samuelson Nobel Prize in Economics, 1970** Market prices are the best estimates of value. Price changes follow random patterns and future share prices are unpredictable.
1965	Michael Jensen conducted the first major study to indicate active managers underperform the indices.

1967	**James Tobin Nobel Prize in Economics, 1981** Separation Theorem: shift the focus from security selection to portfolio structure. He described the theory of diversification in layman's terms by saying: "You know, don't put your eggs in one basket." Headline writers around the world wrote about the Economist, who won the Nobel Prize for saying, 'Don't put eggs in one basket.' "
1970	Eugene F. Fama of the University of Chicago conducted extensive research on stock price patterns and developed the Efficient Markets Hypothesis. It asserts that prices reflect values and information accurately and quickly. It is difficult if not impossible to capture returns in excess of market returns without taking greater than market levels of risk. Investors cannot identify superior stocks using fundamental information or price patterns.
1977	Roger Ibbotson and Rex Sinquefield built an extensive returns database going back to 1926. *Stocks, Bonds, Bills, and Inflation* offered an empirical basis for making asset allocation decisions. It changed the way investors built portfolios.
1973	John McQuown of Wells Fargo Bank in 1971 and Rex Sinquefield of American National Bank in 1973 develop the first passive S&P 500 Index funds.
1973	**Fischer Black, Myron Scholes and Robert Merton; Nobel Prize in Economics, 1997** The development of the Options Pricing Model, which allowed new ways to segment, quantify and manage risk.

1975	The New York Telephone Company invested $40 million in an S&P 500 Index fund to launch the era of indexed investing.
1981	Rolf Banz of the University of Chicago analysed NYSE stocks between 1926-1975. He found that in the long term small companies have higher expected returns than large companies and they behave differently.
1984	With no prediction of interest rates Eugene Fama developed a method of shifting maturities that identifies optimal positions on the fixed interest yield curve.
1985	**Merton Miller and Franco Modigliani Nobel Prizes in Economics in 1990** A theorem relating corporate finance to returns. A firm's value is unrelated to its dividend policy, which is an unreliable guide for stock selection.
1990	**William Sharpe Nobel Prize in Economics, 1990** Capital Asset Pricing Model: The theoretical model defines risk as volatility relative to the market. A stock's cost of capital (the investor's expected return) is proportional to the stock's risk relative to the market.
1993	Eugene Fama and Kenneth French, of the University of Chicago, improve on the single-factor asset pricing model (CAPM). They identify market, size, and value factors in returns to develop the three-factor asset-pricing model.

1994	Richard Thaler publishes *The Winner's Curse*, which signalled the arrival of behavioural economics. Thaler showed that we frequently err when making simple calculations and have trouble with self-control.
1995	Steven L. Heston, K. Geert Rouwenhorst, and Roberto E. Wessels find evidence of higher average returns for small companies in twelve international markets.
2002	**Daniel Kahneman Nobel Prize in Economics for his work on Prospect theory.** Daniel Kahneman, Amos Tversky and other psychologists had worked from 1973 to establish a cognitive basis for common human errors and biases, judgment, decision making and behavioural economics.
2004	Finn E. Kydland and Edward C. Prescott Arizona; Nobel Prize for their work on a new theory on business cycles and economic policy laying the groundwork for more robust models by regarding business cycles as the collective outcome of countless forward-looking decisions regarding consumption, investments, labour supply, etc

The Efficient Market Hypothesis developed in the early 1960s. It began with an observation that price changes of stocks appear to follow 'a random walk'. Also, prices on stocks, bonds or property etc already reflect all the information that is known, and prices instantly change when there is new information.

According to the hypothesis it is impossible to consistently outperform the market by using any information that the market already knows, except through luck.

All this was widely accepted until the late 1990s when behavioural finance research began to clash with the hypothesis. Although the efficient market hypothesis may not be perfect it still offers the most practical basis from which to construct a portfolio.

I am not sure that the two schools clash at all, and it is useful to have an awareness of the investment behaviours that let us down. There are numerous scientific papers published about the way we act against ourselves.

We hate losses

Amos Tversky and Daniel Kahneman's prospect theory[5] explains that we have a tendency to strongly prefer avoiding a loss than we have to acquiring gains. Some studies have suggested that psychologically, losses are twice as powerful as gains. Investment psychologists called this behaviour Loss Aversion. This is the tendency to feel disproportionately more pain by losing money than you would feel satisfaction in gaining an equal amount of money.

In simple terms, their work confirms we find it very unsettling to see our investments go down in value. If an investment makes 20% we are 'quite' pleased but if an investment loses 20% it is easy to panic.

We have a tendency to take on more risk in an attempt to recoup losses. One of the most famous examples of this was

---

5 Kahneman subsequently won the Nobel Prize for Economics

the rogue trader Nick Leeson, who brought down Barings Bank in 1995 when he was found to have lost $1.3 billion. His initial success was followed by large failures, which developed into recklessness and massive risks. His behaviour was tied up with what is called the 'sunk cost' fallacy. Having lost millions, he had to trade with higher stakes or the original stake would have been 'wasted'.

However, the vast majority of investors are more likely to sell profitable shares rather than the underperformers they own,[6] even though there may be a tax planning advantage in creating a loss to offset a gain. We hate the idea of losses.

Anchoring is a term used to describe an investor's tendency to focus on the price paid for an investment and refusing to sell it below this price, or refusing to sell, until it gets back to its best ever price after a fall.

Such decisions are emotional and have nothing to do with an analysis of the investment. A good question is, "If I didn't own the investment would I buy it now?" If the answer is no, then perhaps it should be sold.

We like round numbers

Investors often attach too much attention to meaningless investment indicators. For example, more attention is paid to the FTSE 100 index passing through the 'psychological' 5,000 or 6,000 barriers than they do from it passing through 4,903 or 5,764, because we like round numbers.

---

6 'Are investors reluctant to realize their losses?' Journal of finance Vo LIII No 5 Oct 1998: Terrance Odean Professor of Banking and Finance at the Haas School of Business

There is often the thought of a great opportunity to double your money when the share of a company has halved in value. There is often no reason why it should ever recover because it may have changed forever.

Short-term memories

We attach more importance to recent events than we do to distant events. When technology stocks were racing ahead during the dotcom boom, and then property in the 'buy to let' boom, too many people presumed that the enormous gains would continue forever, forgetting the fact that big downturns have happened in the more distant past.

Short on information

Investors often act on too little information, we can be over-confident about our abilities, and we believe too readily what others tell us without looking for proof.

Our decision-making behaviour can change very quickly on very little information. We use emotions to make investing decisions and these are often illogical and unreliable. We make judgments based on our own recollections, and we often limit ourselves to the information that we already know, or that which is readily available, rather than examining other options.

Also, people often make investment decisions based on the perceived similarity between the current situation and other similar situations they have experienced.

When we learn to recognise these failures in ourselves we can avoid all the unnecessary costs of high volume trading for no benefit.

It takes 16 years to prove investment skill

THERE IS a mathematical proof to demonstrate why it takes 16 years to determine that a manager's excess returns are either down to luck or skill. A manager's apparent skill is measured by what is known as the information ratio (IR) being active return / active risk (alpha / tracking error).

Leading managers exhibit information ratios of around 0.5. The length of time required to discern skill from luck is defined by an equation:

$$\text{Time} = (2 / \text{IR})\, 2, \text{ where '2' is the t-statistic at a 95\% confidence level.}$$

Applying this formula, a fund manager needs a track record of 16 years to be able to prove they were not just lucky. Unfortunately, the number of managers still with the same company after 16 years is minuscule. To follow him or her around costs money because you must sell one fund and buy into another, which eats into any outperformance above the market return. There could also be tax implications.

Active fund management can beat the passive approach, but there is no defined process where we can reliably distinguish in advance between the flops and the flyers.

This part of the argument is easy to understand because we are trying to find an accurate way of reliably predicting the future, which is clearly impossible.

Who could have predicted all the changes to the FTSE 100 index over the years, which is a true measure of corporate success and failure? Surely you must have knowledge of all these businesses if you are going to select one above another and claim to be skilful.

The mature reader will appreciate the names that were once so familiar in our everyday lives and that are now filed away in our distant memories. In twenty years time the index will look just as different again and how could we have kept up with all the changes and begin to separate the future wheat from the chaff?

Date	Added	Deleted
19-Jan-84	CJ Rothschild	Eagle Star
02-Apr-84	Lonrho	Magnet Sthrns.
02-Jul-84	Reuters	Edinburgh Inv. Trust
02-Jul-84	Woolworths	Barrat Development
19-Jul-84	Enterprise Oil	Bowater Corporation
01-Oct-84	Willis Faber	Wimpey (George)
01-Oct-84	Granada Group	Scottish & Newcastle
01-Oct-84	Dowty Group	MFI Furniture
04-Dec-84	Brit. Telecom	Matthey Johnson
02-Jan-85	Dee Corporation	Dowty Group
02-Jan-85	Argyll Group	Berisford (S.& W.)
02-Jan-85	MFI Furniture	RMC Group
02-Jan-85	Dixons Group	Dalgety
01-Feb-85	Jaguar	Hambro Life
01-Apr-85	Guinness (A)	Enterprise Oil
01-Apr-85	Smiths Inds.	House of Fraser
01-Apr-85	Ranks Hovis McD.	MFI Furniture
01-Jul-85	Abbey Life	Ranks Hovis McD.
01-Jul-85	Debenhams	I.C. Gas

Date	Added	Deleted
06-Aug-85	Bnk. Scotland	Debenhams
01-Oct-85	Habitat	Mothercare Lonrho
02-Jan-86	Scottish & Newcastle	Rothschild (J)
08-Jan-86	Storehouse Habitat	Mothercare
08-Jan-86	Lonrho	B.H.S.
01-Apr-86	Wellcome	EXCO International
01-Apr-86	Coats Viyella	Sun Life Assurance
01-Apr-86	Lucas	Harrisons & Crosfield
01-Apr-86	Cookson	Group Ultramar
21-Apr-86	Ranks	Hovis McD. Imperial Group
22-Apr-86	RMC Group	Distillers
01-Jul-86	British Printing & Comms. Corp	Abbey Life
01-Jul-86	Burmah Oil	Bank of Scotland
01-Jul-86	Saatchi & S.	Ferranti International
01-Oct-86	Bunzl	Brit. & Commonwealth
01-Oct-86	Amstrad	BICC
01-Oct-86	Unigate	Smiths Industries
09-Dec-86	British Gas	Northern Foods
02-Jan-87	Hillsdown	Holdings Argyll Group
02-Jan-87	I.C. Gas	Burmah Oil
02-Jan-87	TSB Group	Lucas Industries
01-Apr-87	Argyll Group	Willis Faber
01-Apr-87	Brit. & Commonwealth	Scottish & Newcastle
01-Apr-87	British Airways	Hammerson Properties
27-Apr-87	Next	I.C. Gas
01-Jul-87	Rolls Royce	GKN
01-Jul-87	Hammerson Properties	Lonrho
01-Oct-87	BAA	Unigate
01-Oct-87	Rothmans Intl.	RMC Group
01-Oct-87	Blue Arrow	Saatchi & Saatchi
04-Jan-88	Lonrho	Blue Arrow
04-Jan-88	Scottish & Newcastle	Jaguar
25-Feb-88	Enterprise Oil	Britoil
05-Apr-88	Williams Holdings	Bunzl
05-Apr-88	Burmah Oil	Dixons Group

Date	Added	Deleted
05-Apr-88	Blue Arrow	Sedgwick
05-Apr-88	RMC Group	Standard & Chartered
01-Jul-88	Lucus Industries	Globe Investment Trust
07-Jul-88	Abbey Life	Rowntree
03-Oct-88	LASMO	Blue Arrow
21-Dec-88	British Steel	Abbey Life
03-Jan-89	Standard & Chartered	Next
03-Jan-89	Ultramar	Williams Holdings
03-Apr-89	BICC	Amstrad
03-Apr-89	Carlton Communications	British & Commonwealth
03-Apr-89	Harrisons & Crosfield	Coats Viyella
03-Apr-89	Taylor Woodrow	Storehouse
17-Jul-89	Abbey National	Gateway Corporation
27-Jul-89	Smithkline Beecham	Beecham Group
08-Aug-89	GKN Cons.	Gold Fields
11-Sep-89	Siebe	Plessey
02-Oct-89	Polly Peck Intl.	Harrisons & Crosfield
02-Jan-90	Globe Investment Trust	Granada Group
02-Jan-90	Thames Water	Siebe
02-Apr-90	North West Water	ECC Group
02-Jul-90	Harrisons & Crosfield	Cookson Group
13-Jul-90	Wiggins Teape Appleton	Globe Investment Trust
01-Oct-90	Severn Trent	Burton Group
01-Oct-90	Anglian Water	Carlton Communications
01-Oct-90	Bank of Scotland	Taylor Woodrow
02-Oct-90	Dalgety	Polly Peck
02-Jan-91	Eurotunnel	BPB Industries
02-Jan-91	Willis Corroon	Standard & Chartered
23-Jan-91	Tate & Lyle	STC
02-Apr-91	National Power	Dalgety
02-Apr-91	PowerGen	GKN
02-Apr-91	Williams Holdings	Burmah Castrol
01-Jul-91	Scottish Power Ranks	Hovis McD.
01-Jul-91	Inchcape	Harrisons & Crosfield
01-Jul-91	Rentokil	Hammerson Properties
16-Sep-91	Vodafone Group	Racal Electronics

IT TAKES 16 YEARS TO PROVE INVESTMENT SKILL

Date	Added	Deleted
01-Oct-91	Northern Foods	Ultramar
26-Nov-91	NFC	Hawker Siddeley
04-Dec-91	Smith (W.H.)	Maxwell Communications
02-Jan-92	Tomkins	ASDA Group
02-Jan-92	MB-Caradon	Lucus Industries
02-Jan-92	Laporte	BICC
01-Apr-92	ECC Group	Lonrho
01-Apr-92	Bowater	Royal Insurance
01-Apr-92	Siebe	Trafalgar House
01-Apr-92	Coats Viyella	Tarmac
22-Jun-92	Carlton Communications	Laporte
22-Jun-92	Royal Insurance	Eurotunnel
22-Jun-92	Granada Group	MEPC
13-Jul-92	HSBC Holdings	Midland Bank
21-Sep-92	TI Group Willis	Corroon
21-Sep-92	Scottish Hydro	Pilkington
21-Sep-92	Southern Electric	Royal Insurance
21-Sep-92	Burmah Castrol	Hillsdown Holdings
21-Sep-92	De La Rue	British Aerospace
21-Sep-92	Kwik Save Group	RMC Group
21-Dec-92	Royal Insurance	BET
21-Dec-92	Standard Chartered	Rolls Royce
22-Mar-93	ASDA Group	Smith (W.H.)
01-Jun-93	Zeneca Group	English China Clays
21-Jun-93	British Aerospace	Fisons
21-Jun-93	RMC Group	Kwik Save Group
21-Jun-93	Warburg S.G.	LASMO
21-Jun-93	Wolseley	Southern Electric
20-Sep-93	MEPC	De La Rue
20-Sep-93	Rolls Royce	Tate & Lyle
20-Sep-93	Schroders	Scottish Hydro
25-Oct-93	Southern Electric	Rothmans International
05-Nov-93	Caradon Plc	MB-Caradon
20-Dec-93	Eastern Electricity	Northern Foods
20-Dec-93	Scottish Hydro Electricity	NFC
21-Mar-94	De La Rue	Schroders

Date	Added	Deleted
21-Mar-94	Tarmac	Scottish Hydro
21-Mar-94	NFC	Anglian Water
20-Jun-94	GKN	Tarmac
19-Sep-94	Schroders	NFC
19-Sep-94	3I Group	Coats Viyella
19-Dec-94	**No Constituent Changes**	
17-Mar-95	Tate & Lyle	Wellcome
20-Mar-95	**No Constituent Changes**	
19-Jun-95	**No Constituent Changes**	
26-Jul-95	Cookson Group	Warburg SG Group
18-Sep-95	British Sky Broadcasting Group	Caradon
18-Sep-95	Fisons	MEPC
18-Sep-95	LASMO	United Biscuits
19-Sep-95	Midlands Electricity	Eastern Group
23-Oct-95	London Electricity	Fisons
11-Dec-95	National Grid Group plc	Inchcape plc
18-Dec-95	Pilkington plc	Arjo Wiggins Appleton plc
18-Dec-95	Burton Group plc	London Electricity plc
18-Dec-95	Smiths Industries plc	De La Rue plc
18-Dec-95	Argos plc	Sears plc
18-Dec-95	Foreign & Col Invest Trust	Midlands Electricity plc
28-Dec-95	Dixons Group	TSB Group
31-Jan-96	Greenalls Group plc	Forte plc
13-Mar-96	**No Constituent Changes**	
24-Jun-96	United News & Media	Foreign & Col Inv Trust
24-Jun-96	Orange	Greenalls Group
24-Jun-96	Next	REXAM (formerly Bowater Group)
18-Jul-96	Royal & Sun Alliance Insurance Group plc	Sun Alliance Group plc
18-Jul-96	Railtrack	Royal Insurance
17-Aug-96	Thorn plc	Thorn EMI plc
17-Aug-96	EMI Group plc	Cookson Group plc
23-Sep-96	LucasVarity	Thorn
30-Sep-96	Imperial Tobacco Group	Southern Electric
23-Dec-96	Mercury Asset Management	Coutaulds

Date	Added	Deleted
23-Dec-96	Hays	Pilkington
14-Feb-97	Centrica	Williams Holdings
24-Feb-97	Energy Group	Redland
24-Mar-97	British Land	Argos
23-Jun-97	Halifax	Smith & Nephew
23-Jun-97	Alliance & Leicester	Burton Group
22-Sep-97	Norwich Union	Tate & Lyle
22-Sep-97	Billiton	Hanson
22-Sep-97	Woolwich	Imperial Tobacco Group
22-Sep-97	Sun Life & Provincial Holdings	Mercury Asset Management
22-Sep-97	Williams	Burmah Castrol
17-Dec-97	Diageo	Guinness
17-Dec-97	Nycomed Amersham	Grand Metropolitan
22-Dec-97	Mercury Asset Management	RMC Group
22-Dec-97	British Energy	Blue Circle Industries
22-Dec-97	Amvescap	TI Group
24-Dec-97	Blue Circle Industries	Mercury Asset Management
23-Mar-98	Compass	Dixons
21-May-98	Misys	The Energy Group
02-Jun-98	RMC Group	General Accident
22-Jun-98	Stagecoach Holdings	Wolseley
22-Jun-98	WPP Group	Next
08-Sep-98	Allied Zurich	LASMO
08-Sep-98	British American Tobacco	B.A.T. Industries Plc
21-Sep-98	Colt Telecom Group	British Steel
21-Sep-98	Telewest Communications	Rank Group
21-Sep-98	Sema Group	Blue Circle Industries
21-Sep-98	Securicor	RMC Group
21-Sep-98	Southern Electric	Enterprise Oil
16-Dec-98	Scottish & Southern Energy	Southern Electric Plc
21-Dec-98	Imperial Tobacco Group	Misys
21-Dec-98	Dixons Group	Nycomed Amersham
21-Dec-98	Gallaher Group	Sema Group
21-Dec-98	Hanson	British Land Co
04-Feb-99	BTR Siebe	BTR

Date	Added	Deleted
04-Feb-99	Daily Mail & General Trust	Siebe
22-Mar-99	Energis	Gallaher Group
22-Mar-99	South African Breweries	Safeway
22-Mar-99	Misys	Williams
22-Mar-99	EMAP	Tomkins
29-Mar-99	Sema Group Plc	LucasVarity
06-Apr-99	AstraZeneca	Zeneca
10-May-99	Next	Guardian Royal Exchange
21-Jun-99	Anglo American	Next
21-Jun-99	Blue Circle Industries	Sema Group
28-Jul-99	British Steel Plc	Asda Group Plc
20-Sep-99	Old Mutual	Smiths Industries
20-Sep-99	Sage Group	Stagecoach Holdings
20-Sep-99	Sema Group	EMAP
06-Oct-99	Corus Group	British Steel
11-Nov-99	Logica Plc	Securicor Plc
24-Nov-99	Wolseley Plc	Orange Plc
30-Nov-99	Marconi	General Electric Company
20-Dec-99	ARM Holdings	Severn Trent
20-Dec-99	CMG	British Energy
20-Mar-00	Kingston Communications	NatWest
20-Mar-00	Cable & Wireless	Associated British Foods
20-Mar-00	Freeserve	Allied Domecq
20-Mar-00	Thus	Hanson
20-Mar-00	Baltimore Technologies	Whitbread
20-Mar-00	Psion	Scottish & Newcastle
20-Mar-00	Nycomed Amersham	PowerGen
20-Mar-00	Celltech Group	Thames Water
20-Mar-00	Capita Group	Imperial Tobacco Group
20-Mar-00	EMAP	Wolseley
12-May-00	Allied Domecq	Cable & Wireless Communications Plc
30-May-00	Associated British Foods	Norwich Union Plc
19-Jun-00	Bookham Technology	Kingston Communications

Date	Added	Deleted
19-Jun-00	Hanson	Psion
19-Jun-00	Ocean Group (now Exel)	Thus
19-Jun-00	Scottish & Newcastle	Baltimore Technologies
12-Jul-00	PowerGen Plc	SLPH
27-Jul-00	Granada Compass	Granada Group
27-Jul-00	Imperial Tobacco	Compass Group
18-Sep-00	Granada Media Associated	British Foods
18-Sep-00	Dimension Data Holdings	Hanson
18-Sep-00	Electrocomponents	Rolls Royce
18-Sep-00	Spirent	Scottish & Newcastle
18-Sep-00	Baltimore Technologies	Corus Group
17-Oct-00	Canary Wharf Group	Allied Zurich
23-Oct-00	P & O Princess Cruises PLC	P & O
23-Oct-00	Lattice Group PLC	Freeserve
26-Oct-00	Shire Pharmaceuticals	Woolwich
18-Dec-00	Smiths Group	Baltimore Technologies
18-Dec-00	Associated British Foods	EMAP
18-Dec-00	Autonomy Corporation	Sema
18-Dec-00	Rolls Royce	P & O Princess Cruises
18-Dec-00	Safeway	Bookham Technology
27-Dec-00	Hanson	Glaxo Wellcome
27-Dec-00	GlaxoSmithKline	SmithKline Beecham
02-Feb-01	Compass Group	Granada Compass
02-Feb-01	Granada	Granada Media
19-Mar-01	Sema	Exel
19-Mar-01	Scottish & Newcastle	Autonomy Corporation
10-Apr-01	Morrison Supermarkets	Sema
18-Jun-01	Next	Railtrack Group
12-Jul-01	Smith & Nephew PLC	Blue Circle Industries
07-Aug-01	Brambles Industries	Dimension Data Holdings
10-Sep-01	Gallaher Group	Bank of Scotland
10-Sep-01	HBOS	Halifax Group
24-Sep-01	Friends Provident	Carlton Communication
24-Sep-01	Enterprise Oil	Misys

Date	Added	Deleted
24-Sep-01	Wolseley	CMG
24-Sep-01	Severn Trent Colt	Telecom Group
24-Sep-01	British Land Co	Telewest Communications
24-Sep-01	Man Group	Energis
24-Sep-01	Northern Rock	Spirent
24-Sep-01	Innogy Holdings	Marconi
19-Nov-01	BT Group	British Telecommunications
19-Nov-01	mmO2	United Business Media
24-Dec-01	P&O Princess Cruises	GKN
18-Mar-02	Corus Group	Celltech
10-May-02	Exel	Enterprise Oil
29-May-02	GKN PLC	Innogy Hldgs
24-Jun-02	Johnson Matthey	ARM Holdings
24-Jun-02	Xstrata	Electrocomponents
24-Jun-02	Bunzl	Logica
02-Jul-02	Bradford & Bingley	Powergen
23-Sep-02	Rexam	British Airways
23-Sep-02	Tomkins	EMI Group
23-Sep-02	Alliance Unichem	International Power
21-Oct-02	Emap	Lattice
23-Dec-02	Liberty International	Brambles Industries
23-Dec-02	British Airways	Cable & Wireless
23-Dec-02	Whitbread	Corus Group
24-Mar-03	Kelda Group	Rolls Royce
24-Mar-03	Foreign & Col Invest Trust	British Airways
24-Mar-03	Provident Financial	Royal & Sun Alliance Insurance Group
24-Mar-03	Cable & Wireless	Invensys
11-Jun-03	Rolls Royce	Capita Group
11-Jun-03	Royal & Sun Alliance	Hays
19-Sep-03	Yell Group	Kelda Group
19-Dec-03	British Airways	Provident Financial
19-Dec-03	Hays	Mitchells & Butlers
08-Mar-04	Antofagasta	Safeway
19-Mar-04	Enterprise Inns	Foreign & Col Inv Trust

Date	Added	Deleted
08-Apr-04	William Hill	Amersham
18-Jun-04	Capita Group	GKN
17-Sep-04	Cairn Energy	Bradford & Bingley
16-Nov-04	Corus Group	Abbey National
17-Dec-04	Tate & Lyle	Tomkins
18-Mar-05	International Power	Cairn Energy
17-Jun-05	BPB	Corus Group
17-Jun-05	Hammerson	Bunzl
15-Jul-05	Royal Dutch Shell A&B	Shell Transport & Trading Co
20-Jul-05	Kelda Group	Allied Domecq
16-Sep-05	Partygaming	Hays
16-Sep-05	Cairn Energy	Emap
08-Dec-05	P&O	BPB
13-Dec-05	Brambles Industries	Exel
19-Dec-05	Persimmon	Whitbread
19-Dec-05	Kazakhmys	William Hill
26-Jan-06	British Energy Group	O2
08-Mar-06	Corus Group	P&O
08-Mar-06	**No Constituent Changes**	
07-Jun-06	Vedanta Resources	Daily Mail & General Trust
07-Jun-06	Lonmin	Cable & Wireless
07-Jun-06	Drax Group	Ladbrokes
30-Jun-06	ICAP	BAA
31-Jul-06	Slough Estates	None
05-Sep-06	Bradford & Bingley	BOC
15-Sep-06	Standard Life	Rentokil
15-Sep-06	Resolution	Schroders
11-Oct-06	Experian Group	GUS
11-Oct-06	Home Retail Group	Partygaming
27-Nov-06	Cable & Wireless	Brambles Industries
15-Dec-06	Whitbread	British Energy Group
16-Mar-07	Daily Mail & General Trust	Cairn Energy
30-Mar-07	Schroders	Corus Group
17-Apr-07	Punch Taverns	Gallaher Group
20-Apr-07	Mitchells & Butlers	Scottish Power

Dated	Added	Deleted
18-Jun-07	Barratt Developments	Bradford & Bingley
26-Jun-07	British Energy Group	Alliance Boots
22-Aug-07	Rentokil Initial	Hanson
24-Sep-07	Tallow Oil	Drax Group
24-Sep-07	Taylor Wimpey	Segro
24-Sep-07	Carphone Warehouse	Kelda Group
04-Dec-07	London Stock Exchange	Invesco Plc
20-Dec-07	AMEC	Imperial Chemical Industries
24-Dec-07	Cairn Energy	Punch Taverns
24-Dec-07	First Group	Tate & Lyle
24-Dec-07	TUI Travel	Daily Mail & General Trust
24-Dec-07	Kelda Group	DSG International
24-Dec-07	Admiral Group	Mitchells & Butlers
24-Dec-07	G4S	Barratt Developments
24-Dec-07	Thomas Cook Group	Northern Rock
26-Mar-08	Eurasian Natural Resources	Taylor Wimpey
26-Mar-08	Tate & Lyle	Yell Group
26-Mar-08	Cobham	Rentokil Initial
28-Apr-08	Wood Group (John)	Scottish & Newcastle
30-Apr-08	Bunzl	Resolution
23-Jun-08	Invensys	Alliance & Leicester
23-Jun-08	Ferrexpo	Persimmon
23-Jun-08	Petrofac	Home Retail Group
23-Jun-08	Drax Group	Tate & Lyle
22-Sep-08	Autonomy Corporation	Carphone Warehouse Group
22-Sep-08	Fresnillo	Enterprise Inns
22-Sep-08	Inmarsat	Ferrexpo
22-Sep-08	Stagecoach Group	ITV
22-Dec-08	Amlin	Fresnillo
22-Dec-08	Home Retail Group	Lonmin
22-Dec-08	Randgold Resources	Petrofac
22-Dec-08	Serco Group	Stagecoach Group
22-Dec-08	Tate & Lyle	Wood Group (John)
09-Mar-09	Fresnillo	Tate & Lyle

Dated	Added	Deleted
09-Mar-09	Lonmin	London Stock Exchange Gp
09-Mar-09	Petrofac	Wolseley
09-Mar-09	Intertek Group	First Group
09-Mar-09	F&C Investment Trust	3i Group
09-Jun-09	Wolseley	Drax Gp
09-Jun-09	3i Group	Amin
09-Jun-09	London Stock Exchange Gp	Whitbread
09-Sep-09	Segro	Balfour Beatty
09-Sep-09	Whitbread	F&C Investment Gp
09-Sep-09	Rentokil Initial	Pennon Group
09-Dec-09	Aggreko	Rentokil Initial
09-Dec-09	Balfour Beatty	HBOS

List of Charts and data sources

Page	Chart / Table Title
26	**Do not judge an investment by its past performance** Source: Morningstar IMA UK All Companies sector, only funds with five-year history used, in GBP, net returns, offer to offer price). Source and copyright ©1996-2008 Morningstar Limited. All rights therein are reserved.
59	**Chart to show the frequency of Bull and Bear Markets** FTSE data published with the permission of FTSE. Bull and bear markets are defined in hindsight using cumulative monthly returns. A bear market (1) begins with a negative monthly return, (2) must achieve a cumulative return less than or equal to -10%, and (3) ends at the most negative cumulative return prior to achieving a positive cumulative return. All data points, which are not considered part of a bear market, are designated as a bull market. Chart based on the author's interpretation of material distributed by Dimensional Fund Advisors Ltd.
93	**Investment returns relative to inflation (% pa)** 10 year data FT publications. FTSE data published with the permission of FTSE. 20, 50, and 109 year

LIST OF CHARTS AND DATA SOURCES

data to 2008 – source Barclays Capital – The Equity Gilt study 2009.

94   **The reward for holding equities over a number of consecutive years**
Data to 2008 – source Barclays Capital – The Equity Gilt study 2009

112   **Performance of the FTSE All-Share Index**
FTSE data published with the permission of FTSE

134   **A stock market fund 20 years to 2009**
FTSE data published with the permission of FTSE

135   **The Growth of £1,000 – 20 years to 2009**
Source of data for calculation – FTSE data. FTSE data published with the permission of FTSE

137   **The 50/50 portfolio return**
FTSE data published with the permission of FTSE. Source of inflation data: Office for National Statistics. Source of data for calculation – FTSE data. FTSE data published with the permission of FTSE.

138   **Chart of the 20-year period ending 2009**
FTSE data published with the permission of FTSE. Source of inflation data: Office for National Statistics. Source of data for calculation – FTSE data. FTSE data published with the permission of FTSE.

139   **20 years to Dec 2009 – the best and worst years**
FTSE data published with the permission of FTSE. Source of inflation data: Office for National Statistics. Source of data for calculation – FTSE data. FTSE data published with the permission of FTSE.

141 **The strategies compared – 1990-2009**
FTSE data published with the permission of FTSE. Source of inflation data: Office for National Statistics. Source of data for calculation – FTSE data. FTSE data published with the permission of FTSE. Typical investor experience calculated by the author and based on research findings of John Bogle and of Lukas Schneider.

172 **UK value and small company investing 20-years to 2008**
Source DFA. Data sourced internally at Dimensional Fund Advisors from Dimensional's Returns Program. 2.0. Value stocks are defined as above the 30th percentile in book-to-market ratio. Growth stocks are defined as below the 70th percentile in book-to-market ratio.

Simulations are free-float weighted both within each country and across all countries. UK data provided by London Business School/Style Research.

173 **Global investing 20-years to 2008**
Source DFA. Data sourced internally at Dimensional Fund Advisors from Dimensional's Returns Program. 2.0. Value stocks are defined as above the 30th percentile in book-to-market ratio. Growth stocks are defined as below the 70th percentile in book-to-market ratio.

Simulations are free-float weighted both within each country and across all countries. Europe data provided by London Business School/StyleResearch. US value and growth data provided by Fama/French.

index

Useful contacts and addresses

THE FOLLOWING list shows a number of index fund providers that are available to the public. This list is not complete as there are new entrants to the market every year.

Aviva – www.aviva.co.uk/savings-and-investments/

Aviva Life & Pensions UK Ltd. 2 Rougier Street, York, YO90 1UU Tel. 0800 056 3542

Aviva Index Linked Gilt, Aviva UK Index Tracking (FTSE UK All share index), Aviva International Index Tracking (FTSE World (exUK) Index), Aviva Inv Blue Chip Tracking 1

Barclays Global Investors – www.barclaysglobal.com

Murray House, 1 Royal Mint Court, London EC3N 4HH Tel. 020 7668 8000

BlackRock Continental European Equity Tracker, BlackRock BlackRock Japan Equity Tracker, BlackRock North American Equity Tracker, BlackRock Pacific ex Japan Equity Tracker, BlackRock UK Equity Tracker Fund.

BlackRock see above

Fidelity – www.fidelity.co.uk

Oakhill House, 130 Tonbridge Road, Hildenborough, Tonbridge, Kent TN11 9DZ, United Kingdom. Tel. 0800 414 161

Fidelity Moneybuilder UK Index

DB X-Trackers – www.dbxtrackers.co.uk

A division of Deutsche Bank

FTSE 100 ETF, FTSE 250 ETF, FTSE All Share ETF, Russell 2000 ETF, FTSE All-world Ex UK ETF

Gartmore – www.gartmore.com

Gartmore House, 8 Fenchurch Place, London EC3M 4PB. Tel. 0800 289 33

Gartmore UK Index

HSBC – www.hsbc.co.uk

HSBC Holdings Plc 8 Canada Square, London, E14 5HQ. Tel. 020 7991 8888.

HSBC American Index, HSBC European Index, HSBC FTSE100 Index, HSBC FTSE 250 Index, HSBC FTSE All Share Index, HSBC Japan Index, HSBC Pacific Index

iShares – www.ishares.com

BlackRock Advisors (UK) Ltd, Murray House, 1 Royal Mint Court, London, EC3N 4HH Tel. 0845 357 7000

iShares FTSE 100, iShares FTSE 250, iShares FTSE

developed world ex-UK, iShares FTSE Gilts UK 0-5, iShares FTSE All stocks gilt, iShares FTSEuro first 100, iShares FTSEuro first 80

Legal and General www.legalandgeneral.com/investments/

Legal & General Group Plc. 1 Coleman Street, London, EC2R 5A. Tel. 0800 027 7169

L&G All stocks Index, L&G All Stocks Index Linked Gilt Index, L&G Market Tracker 350, L&G European Index, L&G Global 100 Index, L&G International Index, L&G Japan Index, L&G Pacific Index, L&G UK 100 Index, L&G UK Index, L&G US Index

Lyxor –www.lyxor.co.uk

A division of Societe Generale

Lyxor ETF FTSE 100, Lyxor ETF FTSE 250, Lyxor ETF FTSE All Share, Lyxor ETF MSCI USA, Lyxor ETF MSCI World

M&G- www.mandg.co.uk

Laurence Pountney Hill, London, EC4R 0HH
Tel. 0800 389 8600

M&G European Index Tracker, M&G Index Tracker

Prudential – www.pru.co.uk

Prudential plc, Laurence, Pountney Hill, London, EC4R 0HH
Tel. 0845 783 5500

Pru European Index Tracker, Pru UK Index Tracker

Royal London – www.royal-london.co.uk

55 Gracechurch Street, London, EC3V 0RL, United Kingdom. Tel. 0800 195 1000

Royal London FTSE 350 Tracker

Acknowledgements

I WISH TO thank everyone who encouraged me to write this book. Enough people were told about it when it was still a work in progress to ensure that there was no going back, so I should probably thank modern communications technology as well, even if it isn't conscious of its own existence.

I am grateful for the work of the Noble Laureates and Economists referred to in this book, which over the last decade has enabled me to develop successful long-term investment strategies. Thanks also to those who assisted in translating substantial academic work into practical investment solutions. Thanks to my knowledgeable friends in EBIS in particular.

Gordon Barr has been skilful and sometimes inspirational during his stint as the main editor, and it is good for a father to receive some payback on his son's education!

Thank you to Kirsty Whittaker for taking time out of an impossibly busy schedule to design the cover.

As other writers will acknowledge it is much easier to embark on a project with the support of your loved ones. Thanks to Nathalie for her patience when I was otherwise distracted, her encouragement when the words stopped flowing, and for her valuable ideas.

About the author

MICHAEL HAS spent his entire career in financial services. During this time he has established a strong reputation for integrity and professionalism.

He was the first in his profession in the North West to be awarded the Fellowship of the Personal Finance Society – the highest qualification possible. He is a Chartered Financial Planner, Certified Financial Planner and a Fellow of the Chartered Insurance Institute (Pensions), which is a rare achievement in the industry. He also holds the Advanced Pension qualification, G60, and the Investment Management Certificate.

He is a past winner of the 'Personal Financial Planner' of the year award and a host of other national awards. His clients have not always been aware of these as they judge him more on his ability to provide insightful advice on wealth management, pensions, and tax planning.

Michael is married with two adult sons and he leads an active life.

Index

109 Years of Data 93, 94
1992 Cohorts Series 82

Aberdeen Technology Fund 40
Absolute Return Funds 200
Academic Evdence 32, 33, 73, 164, 161
Active Management 16, 31, 45, 82, 102, 117, 126, 151, 174, 187, 188, 205, 207, 215, 236
Actively Managed Funds 33, 117, 179, 181, 189
Actuarial Experience of Mortality 82
Albert Einstein 130
Amos Tversky 101, 210, 211
Annuity 83, 84, 182
Art 107
Asset Class 18, 142
Australian Financial Services Authority 36
Average Life Expectancy 31, 80
Aviva 231

Bank Charges 97
Bank of England 93, 105, 168, 174
Bank of England Base Rate 93, 174
Banking/banks 18, 23, 29, 31, 45, 47, 49, 51, 52, 53, 58, 64, 68, 73, 105, 110, 133, 212
Bankrupt 109
Barclays Capital 229
Barclays Global Investors 231
Barclays Life Managed fund 34

Base Rate 93, 174
Basil Fawlty 23
Bear Markets 228
Barings 212
Behaviour 16, 25, 29, 30, 57, 101, 106, 107, 116, 131, 140, 211, 212, 213
Benchmark 82, 143, 169, 188
Bernard Madoff 23
Best Performing Fund 26
Bonds 18, 43, 58, 72, 93, 125, 126, 130, 133, 174, 175, 183, 187, 190, 194, 198, 208, 210
Building Society 48, 90, 151
Bull Markets 59, 107, 228
Burton Malkiel 121
Buy to Let 198, 201, 213

Capitalism 96
Catastrophe Risk 58, 60
Charles Dickens 47
Child Trust Fund 184, 185
Christmas 46
Citywire 52
Classic Cars 107
Clerical Medical 34
Coin Tosser 28
Commissions 15, 33, 50, 53, 70, 163, 164, 192
Company Risk 99, 100, 117
Compound Interest 130, 131
Crash 101.105, 106, 107, 108, 113, 117, 118
Credit Crunch 51, 53, 58, 61, 96, 99, 101, 117, 201

Daily Telegraph 42
Daniel Kahneman 99, 101, 167, 210
DAX 102
Debt 50, 51, 53, 83, 143, 197
Defensive Investments 60
Dimensional Fund Advisers, DFA 230
Dotcom Bubble 53, 61, 99
Double Top 120
Doubling Time 88

Eagle Star Insurance 128
Edward C. Prescott 210
Emerging Markets Equity Fund 205
Employer pension schemes 182
Endowments 194
Equitable Life 193
Equities 18, 19, 93, 94, 95, 97, 98, 126, 136, 229
Equity Risk Premium 98, 143
Ernest Gellner 32
Eugene Fama 120, 209
European Equity Fund 205
Evidence 24, 25, 28, 32, 33, 35, 36, 37, 39, 73, 95, 118, 120, 128, 164, 170, 184, 206, 210
Expected Returns 144, 209

Faculty and Institute of Actuaries 194
Fair Price 106, 107, 117
Fees 16, 322, 42, 44, 49, 67, 130, 150, 151, 163, 174, 206
Fidelity 26, 232
Final Salary Pension Scheme 182
Financial Times 55, 111
Finn E. Kydland 210
Fischer Black 208
Fitzrovia 117
Forecasting 38, 39, 73, 111, 117, 118, 119, 131, 163
Freakonomics 80
Free Advice 49, 53, 52, 54, 68, 69, 71, 73, 163

Friends Provident 34, 61, 223
FSA 29, 31, 33, 35, 37, 40, 54, 61, 66, 193, 203
FSA's Register 164
FTSE 100 Index 127, 128, 188, 199, 212, 216
FTSE All Share Index 29, 34, 102, 127, 133, 140, 169, 179, 188, 189, 229, 232
Fund Manager Pay 42
Fund Managers Failures 41
Fund of Funds 193, 205, 206
Future Performance 25, 27, 36, 73

Gartmore 232
Gearing 198
GEB's 200
Gifted Fund Managers 37
Gilts 18, 19, 92, 93, 94, 95, 98, 111, 174, 175, 183, 233
Government Expenditure 82
Guaranteed Equity Bonds 198
Guaranteed Stock Market 193, 198

Hedge Funds 193, 201, 200, 202
Henderson Group 41
High Income 83, 90, 199
High Risk 42, 43, 47, 52, 56, 64, 97, 199, 201, 203
Historical Data 102, 145
Home Bias 143
House of Commons 33
HSBC 23, 34, 48, 219, 232
HSBC Life 34

Income Funds 43
Index Investing 16, 129, 181
Index-Linked Gilts 18, 92, 93, 183
Index-Linked National Savings Certificates 92
Inflation 87, 89
Inherited Money 51
Innovative Technologies 96

INDEX

Insurance 11, 15, 18, 19, 29, 31, 45, 47, 55, 56, 58, 60, 61, 64, 68, 70, 73, 83, 84, 128, 133, 191, 192, 193, 194, 195, 219, 220, 224, 236
Interest Rates 25, 72, 92, 93, 99, 131, 174, 175, 198, 209
Investment Bonds 18
Investment Returns 41, 62, 65, 67, 72, 93, 143, 188, 228
Investment Skill 215, 219, 221, 223, 225, 000
Investment Trusts 19
Investors Chronicle 121
IQ 166, 167
ISA, ISA Allowance 190
iShares 19, 232, 233

James Tobin 208
John Bogle 141, 230
John Maynard Keynes 86, 116
John McQuown 208
Journal of Economic Surveys 120
Journal of Medicine 77

Karl Jung 15
Kenneth French 209
Key Data 200
Keynes 86, 116

L&G, Legal & General 200, 233
Legalised Theft 15, 24, 53
Lehmans 200
Life Span 81, 85
Lincoln Balanced 34
Liverpool Victoria, LV 191
Lloyds TSB 34
London Life 61
Long-dated Bonds 175
Lukas Schneider 141, 230

M&G 233
Managed Funds 17, 19, 33, 35, 36, 102, 117, 179, 181, 189, 195
Market Return 113, 125, 126, 142, 203, 215

Market Risk 99
Means Testing 83
Medicine 77
MFI 128, 216
Million 42, 52, 92, 109, 110, 187, 197, 202, 203, 209
Millionaire Lifestyle 90, 91, 93, 95
Minutes of Evidence, House of Commons 33
Momentum 107, 121
Morningstar 30, 31, 228
Mortgage 50, 51, 52, 53, 152, 198
Mount Vesuvius 57
Mutual Funds 19
Myron Scholes 208

NatWest Bank 52
New Model Adviser 44
New Star 40, 41, 42, 43, 44, 206
New York Telephone Company 209
NHS 83, 85
NHS Budget 85
Nick Leeson 212
Nobel Prize 40, 167, 188, 207-210, 211
NPI 61

OEIC's 18
Options Pricing Model 208
Overend, Gurney & Co 105

Parliament 33, 168
Past Imperfect? 35
Past Performance 25, 26, 27, 30, 33, 35, 36, 37, 39, 40, 43, 45, 73, 174, 179, 228
Paul Samuelson 40, 207
Peloton Hedge Fund 201
Pension Funds 19, 34
Pension schemes -- money purchase 182
Pension schemes -- final salary 182

Pets.com 110
Phoenix Life Exempt 34
Ponzi schemes 23
Portfolio Turnover 117
Premium Bonds 187, 194
Probability 33, 36, 94, 95
Property Fund 41, 44, 183, 196, 197
Prudential, Pru 191, 194, 233

Rebalance 154, 155
Rebalancing 139, 146, 154, 155
Refuge 191
Resistance Level 120
Rex Sinquefield 208
Richard Thaler 210
Robert M. Pirsig 167
Robert Merton 208
Roger Ibbotson 208
Role of the media 45
Rolf Banz 209
Royal London 234

S&P 31, 102, 208, 209
S&P 500 102, 208, 209
Sandler Review 193
Scottish Amicable 61
Scottish Equitable 61
Scottish Life 34
Scottish Mutual 61
Scottish Widows 62
Selling in May 110
Short Term Goals 78, 95, 132
South Sea Bubble 105
Special Allocations 70
Split Strike Conversion 23, 24
St Leger's Day 110
St. Thomas Aquinas 106
Stamps 107
Standard Life 225
State Pension 80, 82, 83, 153
State Retirement Age 81
Stephen Dubner 80

Stock Market Fund 34, 41, 134, 143, 150, 153, 157, 229
Stock Market Investments 18, 60, 94, 155, 193, 198
Structured Products 200
Sun spots 167
Sunk Cost 212
Surgical Safety Checklist 77
Survivors 30, 202
Survivorship Bias 31
Swiss Finance Institute 31
Systematic Risk 99

Tallulah Bankhead 73
Tax 63, 83, 90-93, 101, 133, 162, 182, 190, 193, 195, 196, 204, 205, 212, 215
Tax Return 90, 101, 195
Tech Bubble 51, 194
Technical Analysis 119, 120, 126
Tracker Fund 128, 180, 183, 231
Treasury Bill, T - Bill 143, 174
Treasury Committee 33

UK Equity 27, 34, 35, 231
  Value 30, 170, 172, 174
  Small Cap 30, 170, 172, 174
Unfashionable Stocks 101
Unit Trusts 19, 35, 40, 194
Uptrend 120
US Equity Funds 31

Vanguard 141, 170
Venture Capital Trusts, VCTs 193, 204

Wall Street 40, 121
Weather Forecast 38, 39
Webvan 38, 39, 110
William Sharpe 209
Wine 107
With Profit Funds 193
Worst Performing Fund 26